THE SIBYLS: THE FIRST
OF MAMI (WA

CW00540023

Demystifying the Absence of the African Ancestress
As the First Divine Prophetess on Earth

Mama Zogbé
Chief Hounon-Amengansie

This booklet is part of a series towards the Reclamation of the Religious Heritage
of the Diaspora Project

Mami Wata Healers Society of North America Inc.,
Martinez, GA 30907

Library of Congress Cataloging in Publication Data

Hunter-Hindrew, Vivian
The Sibyls: the First Prophetess' of Mami (Wata)
Demystifying the Absence of the African Ancestress
As the First Divine Prophetess on Earth.
Vivian Hunter-Hindrew
Notes,
Index.
ISBN 0-9716245-6-9.

Requests for such permission should be addressed to:
Mami Wata Healers Society of North America Inc.,

P.O. Box 211281
Martinez, GA 30907
Hqts: (706) 267-3324
Fax: (706) 863-4886
Website: www.mamiwata.com
Email: MWHS@mamiwata.com

Manufactured in the United States of America.
Cover Design: by Mama Zogbé (Vivian Hunter-Hindrew).

The: First Prophetess' of Mami

Vatican: Divining Serpent. Derived from Vatis = *Diviner* and Can = *Serpent*. Vatican City and St. Peter's Basilica were built on the ancient pagan site called in Latin vaticanus mons or vaticanus colli, which means hill or mountain of prophecy."

Hebrew Definition:

Vatic:

1. (*vatis, vates*) a seer, prophet, soothsayer, diviner, divination.

2. Soothsayer: to act covertly, to use hidden arts ie. magic, to practice sorceries, mysteries

3. Diviner means: witchcraft, tell fortunes (fortuneteller), bewitch, to consult a spirit of the dead, to practice magic.

==
Source:

What does the word "Vatican" mean?
https://www.xtreemnews.com/single-post/2017/12/25/What-Does-the-word-Vatican-mean

The Vatican Enforces the Will of the Gods; the Divining Serpent Has the Whole World Deceived
https://yahwehsbranch.com/the-vatican-enforces-the-will-of-the-gods-the-divining-serpent-has-the-whole-world-deceived/

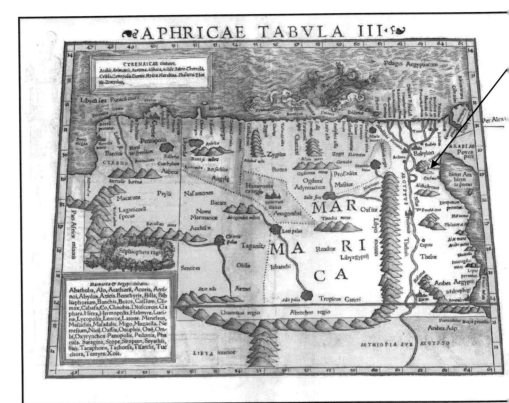

Munster's Geographia 1540 edition map showing the real ancient Babylon located in Southern Egypt (upper rt). Babylon in Egypt has now been removed from modern maps. Munster, a linguist and mathematician, who initially taught Hebrew in Heidelberg, is generally regarded as one of the three most important map makers of the 16th Century.

"Justin tells the Greeks that they may find the true religion in the ancient Babylonian Sibyl, who came to Cuma and there gave her oracles, which Plato admired as divine. Clemens Romanus also quotes the Sibyls in his Epistle to the Corinthians.** They are alsoquoted by Theophilus Antiochenus, Athenagoras, Firmianus, Lactantius, Eusebius, St. Augustine, &c.* Floyer's."   Goffery Higgins, Anacalypsis p.747

NO. 64.—AFRICAN SIBYL.

"It is not surprising that the Cilician terra-cottas, which, we have seen, embrace so large a field of Oriental [East African], Egyptian, Greek, and Roman mythology, should also contain illustrations of oracular beings and virgin [Pagan] prophetesses, who played an important part in the rise of Christianity. Whose books were largely used by the ancient fathers of the Church, . . . against the Pagans, and whose prophecies did not fall before the light of a new religion for nearly four centuries after the advent of Jesus."

Barker, William Burckhardt

FORWARD

THINKING OUTSIDE THE WESTERN PATRIARCHAL BOX

The idea that African religious traditions, ritual practices, social customs, divine prophecy and fundamental beliefs once dominated both the secular and non-secular world in ancient times, seems hard to imagine. Even more, the notion that African women,the oldest human beings on the planet, laid the theological foundation for Judaism, Hinduism, Christianity and Islam under the auspices of the black matriarchs seems even more incredible.

Considering the current status of African women around the world, one could hardly be convinced that her matriarchal presence and the enormous influence she welded in the ancient world, had far exceeded the limited physical, cultural geographical and political designations of which Africa and her religions are confined today. One could hardly imagine too, that African religions had reached very high levels of theological and ritual development. And that they were the original home of the worlds first great oracles, prophetess and prophets. The absence of African women in world history as major players, as oppose to "exceptions to the norm," or mere appendages of 'great men', has been problematic and disturbing at best. For the first time, "herstory" is being unearthed, revealed and told.

FIRST PROPHETESS' IN THE WORLD

The first prophets of Mami (Wata) were African women. They were called "Sibyls", meaning, that they were Mami Wata

iii

priestesses and priests of the *Oannes*. The more advance of this matriarchal divine order are known as *Amegansies* in West Africa today. They can call-up the dead, and even the souls of the living. They were the ancient oracle used in Ancient Greece, Roman and Babylon. Their prophecies are the oldest in the world. It is through the divine blood of these Sibyl priestesses that the patriarchal kingships of the Pharaohs, the Hebrew prophets and the Chaldean priests were born.

THE GREAT SIBYLS: DIVINE ORACLES OF THE ANCESTORS AND GOD

Webster's dictionary defines a Sibyl as "a *female prophet,"* or *"a woman able to utter the oracles and prophecies of a god; or a woman who can foretell the future."* Conversely, under the bitter Hebrew patriarchs, the Sibyls are condemned in their Bible, as *"Behalath-Ob"*, meaning "evil serpent/spirit," or *"mistress of the Python."*

SIBYL: BLACK DOVES ORIGINAL 'HOLY SPIRIT'

Universally known as the *"Black Doves*, the Sibyls referred to themselves as *"Sisters of Isis*, and sometimes *[prophetesses] of the black Di-ana."* The *"doves,"*symbolize the sacred soul, or *"holy spirit."* An Afro- mystical symbol later adopted by the Christians. It was the Sibyls matriarchal groups who settled at Asia Minor (ancient Turkey), and installed Mami's worship, more than 2500 years before the Doric (Greek) and Turk invasions. "Mami" whom they knew as *"Laocoon with her serpents"* was known as the manifestation of the *Divine logos*, with holy temples scattered all thoughout Asia Minor (Cushitic Mitanni Empire) and in Minoa and Mycenae (Aegean Islands).

Archeological pottery shards date the black descendants of the Libyan, Garamantes (present day Ewe/Alladas/ Ga-Adangbe) and other African clans who had settled into ancient Babylon and elsewhere, before the Flood, to have arrived in Minoa (Ionia) as early as 4000 B.C.E. Hailed as one of the *"Seven Wonders of the World"*, these sacred temples were maintained by the Sibyls and a contingent of vestal *"virgin"* priestesses and eunuchs.

VATICAN: ORIGINAL SACERDOTAL SEAT OF SIBYLS

Africans (black Buddhists Umbrians, and black Etruscans etc.,) erected civilizations in what is now Italy, thousands of years before the Anglo-Romans arrived. What is now called the *"seat of the Vatican"* in Italy, was originally the sacerdotal seat of the ancient black Sibyls. As the first established, sacerdotal, African matriarchs, the Sibyls cultural and religious impact was arguably the most profound, on ancient civilization than modern history has ever revealed or care to admit. From Mesopotamia, to Libya, Mizarim (Kemet/Egypt), Ionia, Minoa, Peloponnese (Turkey) and Mycenae (Greece) and later Rome, the Sibyls were the primary, divine Vatican and absolute moral authority.

For centuries, the Grecian islands at *Delos, Dodona, Delphi* and the temple of Mami in ancient Libya, were the ecclesiastical and moral hub of religious, social and international political activity. It was under the theocratic governance of the Sibyls, as Queen Mothers, that African matriarchal culture reached its *"golden age"* of achievement in medicine, religion, astronomy, philosophy, law, architecture, music, art and social sophistication.

SIBYLS: HEAL SICK, RAISE DEAD LONG BEFORE CHRIST

As the sole spiritual authority in the ancient world, the Sibyls were famous for uttering warnings and admonitions to the villages, cities and ancient kingdoms, including their leaders; prophesying their doom, or fulfilling their hopes and restoring lost glory. They'd right moral wrongs and punish offenders of the divine law. Centuries before for Christ, they were known to heal the sick, restore dignity and strength to weak and sight to the blind. They were famous for curing lameness, epileptics, deaf mutes and lepers. They were said to "*cast out demons*" and even to "*raise-up the dead.*" This last reference is probably meant to "*call-up and materialize the spirit of a dead person.*" For example, the A Sibyl named *Herophile*, residing in Cumean, Rome, was famed for calling-up the spirit of the *Apostle Samuel* from the dead.

SIBYLS DIVINE ORACLE BASIS FOR WESTERN BIBLE

However, the Sibyls most significant contribution were their famous oracles containing the divine prophecies that they would utter in trance possession. These prophecies would be carefully written down by their assistants and complied into books. These prophetic proses were the basis for Greek and Roman tragedies and plays. These prophetic books were later collected by the Roman authorities, and soon became the sole and undisputed precursor to the western, Christian Bible, and would later lay the ecclesiastical foundation of Western civilization.

Over the millenniums other Sibyl prophecies, oracles and revelations were systematically retrieved and purchased, stolen or haphazardly collected by various means, all throughout the ancient world where their temples existed.

It was these books that would later be plagiarized, revised or altered, and complied into one "*holy book*" known as the *Sibylline Oracles*. They would later become the center of the bitter "doctrinal or hersey wars" between the waring Levitical Jews, and the emerging Roman Vatican authority. As the African matriarchal power began to decline, and her colonies taken over by foreign conquerors, it was the thrones and sacerdotal power and prophecies of the Sibyls that was stolen from them by the emerging Roman Church. Their religions were later labeled as "pagan/heathen" under a now racialist Roman authority.

The emerging Roman Church in their ignorance and ambition, acquired and doctored the Levite Jews' corrupted versions of the Sibyl prophecies, until one could hardly distinguish one forgery from the other.   Some of these prophetic books were used by the Vatican to compile what is known today as the *Judeo-Christian Bible,* crediting their authorship to conspicuous Roman and other male "prophets." Those books for which it was hard to conceal their African matriarchal origins were simply destroyed, or relegated to heresy.

GENDER OF 'GOD" ORIGINALLY FEMININE

The gender of "*god*" was later changed from feminine to masculine. Originally, within each prophetic verse, it is claimed the Sibyls made praises to "*Mami*" as "*Our Lady*," and proclaimed that she was "*greater than any other [god] in the world*."Roman senator, Cicero,(the orator) writes that the last three books of the Sibyl *Herophile* were deliberately burned in a fire by the Roman Governor, "*Stilicon the Tyrant.*" Stilicon was eternally hated by all of Rome for this sacrilegious act, which prompted a universal reaction from poets, scholars and musicians alike. So worshiped was this Sibyl of Cumea, that she was immortalized by all of Rome in one of her appellations "*Europa*" for which Europe is allegedly named.

SIBYLS GROUPS ORIGINAL "PERSECUTED ONES"

It was this African traditional religionist groups and not the so-called "Christians" who were the actual ones persecuted and finally enslaved. It was the Sibyl's style of prophecy and magic that would later be imitated by a militant faction from these patriarchal, levitical groups whom, envious of her global positioning, rebelled the divine matriarchal orders and seized their temples and overthrew their priestesshood. In their jealousy, hatred and rebellion of her divine authority, the Levitical Jews elevated their original minor deity, "*Jehovah*" as an insult to Her. Together, "*Jehovah*" and his patriarchal clan usurped her sacerdotal and secular power and from that moment on, they have worn it as their own.

Millions of her people were murdered or enslaved, and millions scattered to the four winds all all accorss the world. The historical evidence shows that it was these groups and not the "Christians" who were the actual ones persecuted and finally enslaved. The New Testament is actually a historically chronicle of the final destruction of all remnants of the African matriarchal authority. Books that were politically, and (not divinely) inspired, which is why the Levtical Jews, enemies of the Roman Church, refused to recognize them as authentic.

SIBYL TRADITIONS LIVE-ON IN WEST AFRICA

The history of the Sibyls is not entirely dead. In West Africa there lives a matriarchal order of women who "call-up the dead." Many lineages of these women were also sold into slavery in America.

Many black women are born not knowing that their suffering stems from their disconnection with their ancient rites and spiritual duty to continue the work of their ancient mothers. The suppression of the ancient history of the African matriarchs and their contributions to world religion, magic, spirituality and prophecy is one of the greatest cover-ups and divine tragieis in human history. This author remains convinced that until this history is restored, and African women are accorded their rightful place in the world, their will probably never be any peace.

Mama Zogbé,
Chief Hounon-Amengansie,
Mami Wata, Mama Tchamba, Yeveh Vodoun Religion

THE SIBYLS: THE FIRST PROPHETESS'
OF MAMI

THE SIBYLS: THE FIRST PROPHETESS' OF MAMI

Demystifying the Absence of the African Ancestress
As the First Divine Prophetess on Earth

Fig.1: Above, is a Medieval, Roman catacomb, illustrating a Mami, Sibyl priestess/*Amengansie*, reposed against the sacred Ark/*Omphaé* (ancestral oracle). It is topped with an *Agbandoto* (first fruits offering to Mami). The Omphaé is laced with a garland of mistletoe sacred to the African Thunder god *"Zeus/Aesculapius/Dionysus/ Bacchus"*. Resting in her hand is *Aesculapius*, the African ancestral oracular serpent. Emanating around her head is the golden *nimbus* halo. A pre-Christian, solar symbol representing her *"Muse"* or *"Avatar"* status. The feminine word *"Radha/Muse"* (masculine,*"Moses"*) is the exact same equivalent as *"Messiah/Savior,"* meaning *"bearers of divine truth and light."*[1] Additionally, the word *Mago* is the feminine counterpart to the masc. word *Magi*, *meaning masters of divine spirit and esoteric knowledge.* The use of *mermaid* imagery in the Mami Wata Vodoun tradition has been a dominate feature since the beginning of time. The oldest representations of *Isis/ Mami/Atergatis/Awussa/Densu/ Ishtar* were that of a serpent, fish and mermaid. During ancient times, African and Afro-Elamite matriarchal religions reached high levels of civilization, and its architecture, sacerdotal rites, elaborate vestments, and "orgiastic" (possessions) celebrations covered the entire ancient world. They dominated the religious, political and popular cultures of colonial (and classical) Greece and Rome. The prophecies and wisdom of the Sibyls and other African esoteric priesthoods were central to Christianity's ecclesiastical development and Levitical Judaism's survival. After the militaristic defeat and decline of African, patriarchal world hegemony, the Roman Church began to emerge as an imperialists inquisitorial power. They then exploited and plagiarized the Sibyl prophecies and usurped their sacred rites, and Vatican seat of divine power in Italy. They credited their prophetic works to obscure white, males whom they labeled as *"prophets and saints."* They then waged "holy" war against the Sibyls later accusing them of *"Taurian [black] heathenism"*. The Roman catacombs became the burial mausoleums for many of these persecuted and murdered African martyrs. The Sibyls (and others) were buried by their followers in these dark, musty tombs. Their beloved entering late at night to offer food, drink, prayer and song. The use of undergrounds (an ancient Egyptian and Afro-Chaldean religious custom) can be likened to the slave survival practices in America. They are an important, historical glimpse into the, socio-religious,and political world of the Afro-Greco-Romans, as they fought for their religious and cultural survival.   (Via Latina, Rome, 361-363 C.E.)

In 1935, an important cultural undertaking was instituted, to document and to preserve Afro-medicinal-spiritual folklore and religious practices in America. This monumental task was instituted by the Alma Egan Hyatt Foundation of New York, under the auspices of an Episcopal priest by the name of *Harry Middleton Hyatt.*, from Quincy, Illinois. Mr. Hyatt traveled across the (mainly) Southern, United States interviewing hundreds of ex-enslaved African-American priestesses and priests, and their descendants. He transcribed to ediphones their folklore, folk medicine and religious practices; many of whom, in spite of violent suppression and persecution, still practiced remnants of the religious traditions of their ancient African ancestors. The more than sixteen hundred women and men practitioners interviewed by Mr. Hyatt, anxious to help document and preserve their important religious culture, volunteered to contribute to this historic, archival study.[2] What is interesting to note is that during the course of these interviews, nearly all of the women and an impressive number of the men declared with the strongest conviction, that they were indeed true *"prophets, prophetess and doctors."* Commenting on this and the esoteric nature of black folk-cosmogony, Hyatt remarked:

> What type of thought am I trying to bring above ground where it can be studied ... [is] a continuation of a mental phenomena centuries old, the syncretism of magic[al] rites, pseudo-science and religion. We could call it an underground gnosticism. [3]

A great many of those interviewed claimed that they were prophets/prophetess' because the *"spirits called them"* or because their mothers or fathers came from a *"blood lineage"* of *"two-headed people"*, or because they were simply *"born that way,"* ... *"It's in the blood."*

Now, one might wrongly conclude upon first observation, that since it was illegal for enslaved Africans to either read or write, such bold proclamations could only be due to their "Christian" conditioning. The only "good thing," (being "Christianized") they were taught, that resulted from some 150 years of chattel slavery and *Jim Crow* segregation.

However, a closer examination might reveal that many in the Diaspora may very well have been descendants of the Sibyls, the first prophetess of Mami, the original "God/dess," whose history has been lost, stolen, deliberately culturally disguised obscured and Europeanized beyond recognition in the contemporary faiths of today. However, with an increasing number of African-Americans finding no solace in today's scandal ridden, unfiling western faiths, desire to learn the true history of their ancient ancestral religions that once dominated the world. Therefore, the time is neigh that their story be told.

Introduction

Before there was "Jehovah", a minor volcano/fire/thunder deity elevated as "God" under Afro-Afrim (Jewish) patriarchy, there was Mami/Isis as the preeminent dual Goddess and God who dominated the entire ancient world. For more than 6,000 years, nearly all of Africa was matriarchal. The dominate presence of African matriarchy resulted not as a consequence of political /feminists or military usurpation, but rather because it was the original and (more importantly) the <u>natural divine order</u> of the African civilized world. Its cosmology, philosophy, theology, ritual practices, and rich African culture empathized the complimentary relationship between what has come to be known as the "masculine" and "feminine" divine, as it exists in both nature and within the universe.

What passes for "traditional" African culture today where women have been subdued, and relegated to marginal roles in African political and religious life, is the result of the patriarchal usurpation of the older matriarchal orders upon whom the patriarchs sought to contain and to control her divine powers and political and economic influence. However, hidden beneath this patriarchal substratum of "modern" day Africa, one will discover that it was under African matriarchy which birthed ancient African and Mediterranean culture and high civilization.

The first prophets of Mami were African women. They were called "Sibyls", meaning, that they were Mami Wata priestesses and priests of the Oannes. Their prophecies are the oldest in the world. It is through the divine blood of these Sibyl priestesses that the patriarchal kingships of the Pharaohs, the Hebrew prophets and the Chaldean priests were born. It was the Sibyl's style of prophecy and magic that would later be imitated by a militant faction from these groups, who, envious or her global positioning, rebelled against these divine matriarchal orders and seized their temples and overthrew their priestesshood as patriarchy began to dominate.

In their jealousy, hatred and rebellion of her divine authority, the Levitical Jews elevated their original minor deity, "Jehovah" as an insult to Her. Together, "Jehovah" and his patriarchal clan usurped her sacerdotal and secular power and from that moment on, they have worn it as their own. They did not create a new logos, they simply corrupted and repackaged the original as laid forth by the Divine African Mother.

To conceal their crimes, they destroyed and defiled Her name and all of Her temples. They murdered and accused Her prophetesses and prophets of heresy and witchcraft and disguised her sacred rites and divine legacy as their own. This trend of random destruction they continued, so that the world would never again know or honor Her, as their Divine African Mother.

Since their unauthorized acquisition of Her divine authority, there has been little peace in the world. Because they have demonized the voice of her prophetesses and continue to enslave and oppress her prophets and people, there has been no divine prophecy. All that remains are hopeless corruptions of Her original logos and weak imitators (such as Nostradamus) of Her divine prophetic style, a style originally developed by the Sibyls and those of her sacred priestshoods.

The Jews whom after the fifth century B.C.E. (Forlong) could neither speak nor understand Hebrew, nor the ancient esoteric philosophy of Mami, attempted to decipher the original cuneiform tablets of the black Canaanites that predate the Hebrew language. Their crude translations deliberately corrupted many of the ancient names of the black goddesses, and changed the original esoteric meanings of their prophecies to what exist now in the Torah and in the Pentateuch.

These now corrupted and worn "scriptures/doctrines," mass produced and distributed now in the Judea-Christian bible, have been the cause of untold human suffering, massive spiritual ignorance, spiritual suffering and devastating wars. This was especially the case between those rebellious sons of the patriarchal, Afro-Pharaonic orders, who themselves were overthrown and robbed of their secular hegemony by their illegitimate off-springs- Judaism, Christianity and Islam. Though, all late comers into this very ancient and divine epic, their "holy wars" claiming original ownership of the black, goddess legacy are centuries old, and are all that is allowed to remain within human memory.

Ignorant of the original logos established by the Divine African Mother, their present struggles to maintain the corrupted verison which favors an exclusive (currently Euro-) masculine/patriarchal predominance, are nothing more than a continuation of a centuries old battle over which patriarchal son should control and reign over the sacerdotal power stolen from Her. The most coveted prize, inherent within their secular authority are the spoils of Her vast empire of land and mineral resources, replete with human, carefully programed vassals to exploit.

This sacred empire once bequeathed to the masses, is now controlled by those who have benefitted from Her suspicious absence from human worship as Mami, and the continual subjugation and degradation of the people who have known and have honored her sacred rites and religious customs for centuries; rooted in what are known today as "African traditional and Diaspora religions".

For many ATR (African Traditional Religious) practitioners, this revelation might come as shocking and unbelievable. The idea that African religious traditions, ritual practices, social customs, divine prophecy and fundamental beliefs once dominated both the secular and non-secular world, and laid the theological foundation for Judaism, Hinduism, Christianity and Islam under the auspices of the black matriarchs seems incredible. However, in order to understand what has just been written, it is necessary to start at some historic point in our human beginnings.

Clearly, the first question begs, just "who are the Sibyls," and why have the world not learned of their Africaness, and their primary and sacred role as te world's first prophetess, or their major contribution to the divine history of world religions?

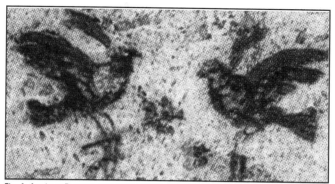

Fig.4: Ancient, Roman catacomb drawing of Sibyls, the "Black Doves," sent out by
Mami (Ishtar)," to test for dry land. Some accounts report that one of them returned
carrying an olive branch, which is credited as being sacred to the black, goddess
"Minerva." She is one of three major serpent water deities born at Lake Triton,
daughter of "Nilus" (the Nile). It was the Africans and Proto-Elamites who settled at
Asia Minor (ancient Turkey), and installed her worship, more than 2500 years before
the Doric (Greek) and Turk invasions. The "doves," symbolize the sacred soul, or
"holy spirit". An Afro- mystical symbol later adopted by the Christians.
St Callistus Catacomb, Rome 199-217 B.C. Bussagali, 1999.

Those "doves" that were sent forth were the "*the black
doves,*"or the transmigrated souls of the Sibyls, whose priestshoods
were already well known and long established in ancient Ethiopia,
Egypt, Mesopotamia and other ancient lands that were spared from
the Great Flood. We know this to be so because Herodotus, who
actually met one of the temple Sibyl priestesses, further recounts
the story directly told to him of how they arrived in their new land
and established the sacred Ompahé temples in Libya and at
Dodona, Delphi and *Delos of the Grecian islands.* He writes that:

*At Dodona . . . the priestesses who delivered the oracles have a story: [that] two black
doves, . . . flew away from Thebes in Egypt, and one of them alighted [landed] at
Dodona, the other in Libya. The former, perched on an oak, and speaking with a human
voice, told them that there, on that very spot, should be an oracle of Zeus [Horus].
Those who heard her understood the words to be a command from heaven, and at
once obeyed. . . the dove which flew to Libya, told the Libyans to found the oracle of*

*Amon [located at the Oasis [at Siwa]. . . which is also an oracle of [the thunder god]
Zeus. The people who gave me this information were the three priestesses at Dodona-
Promeneia the eldest, Timarete the next, and Nicandra the youngest- and their account
is confirmed by the Dodonaeans who have any connection with the temple.[6]*

Other accounts differ on how they arrived in Dodona. It is
said that they were in such high demand throughout the ancient
world, that they were often stolen from Africa, sold as slaves by
the Afro-Phoenicians/Carthaginians and forced to establish their
ancestral and totemic oracles.

On this Herodotus concludes:

I think that, if it be true that the Phoenicians carried off the holy women, and sold them
for slaves . . . Afterwards, while undergoing servitude in those parts, she built under
a real oak a temple . . . Then, having acquired a knowledge of the Greek tongue, she
set up an oracle. She also mentioned that her sister had been sold for a slave into Libya
by the same persons as herself. The Dodonaeans called the women doves because they
were foreigners, and seemed to them to make a noise like birds. After a while the dove
spoke with a human voice . . . by calling the dove black the Dodonaeans indicated that
the woman was an Egyptian. And certainly the character of the oracles at Thebes and
Dodona is very similar. . . It seems to me a sufficient proof . . . that in Egypt these
practices have been established from remote antiquity, while in Greece they are only
recently known. [7]

Quoting archeologists Stecchini, when presenting his findings to
the Archaeological Institute of America, Stecchini states that:

. . . I maintain that the historical accounts, myths, and legends and some monuments
of Delphi, indicate that the oracle was established there by the Pharaohs of the
Ethiopian Dynasty. This is the reasons why the Greeks portrayed Delphos, the
eponymous hero of Delphi, as a Negro.[8]

These written accounts are the only written records
available documenting the historical existence of the Sibyls and
their prophetic oracles. These historical accounts also establish their
existence centuries after their arrival in the new lands, after their
temples had already been seized and renamed i.e., "*Zeus and
Apollo*" by the Pharonic (sun/thunder temple) priests of Amon.

More will be provided on this later. What is more important here is that the first thing the Sibyls and *Ioa* ("*Noah*") did was to construct an Omphaé (temple/shrine) and make sacrifices to Mami. They installed and consecrated the sacred (omphaé) shrines to Mami and their minor gods. This they did in Libya and at Delos, Delphi and Dodona. Afterwards, some of these groups, settled into Asia Minor, (modern day Turkey) and installed a shrine to Mami. Never having broken their ancestral ties with Kemet (Egypt), Nubia, Lybia, Syria and *Pelasheth* (Palestine), they soon developed a sophisticated trade and prospered into what would later become known as the great Minoan and Mycenaean matriarchal civilizations. It was there, legend has it, that became the new abode for their lineage of African Gods. They preserved their history in poetic and prophetic prose that would later be used as the basis for Greek and Roman tragedies and plays, the would lay the ecclesiastical foundation for the collection of apocryphal books later to be modified as the "*Christian*" Bible.

During ancient times, leaders customarily applied allegory and poetic rhyme to conceal, as well as to commit to heart esoteric truths that were not meant for the masses. The priesteshood of the Sibyls were even more conspicuous. They were part of the divine cycle of *Procreation, Preservation, Death and/renewal (rebirth),* which was believed to take place every 600 (6,000) years. The above allegorical story of their arrival upon an Argos/ark with "*Noah*" and his three sons, after surviving the great flood (destruction) is simply representative of this divine cycle.[9]

Another example would be that of the nine Muses (masculine "*Moses*"). Originating out of ancient Egypt, they were the feminine counterpart to the "*Messiah/Savior.*" Each one represented a Sibyl as the divine incarnation of the nine cycles/*Radhas/Rays*, "*divine saviors*" who had already manifested as the new "*Messiah*," of healing and prophecy; and to announce the coming end of a divine cycle.

In short, the *Muses/Sibyls* were literally the *"light of divine wisdom"* or the divine spark of the Divine African Mother as "Mami".

They were symbolically, the divine rays of truth, emanating from the crowns of the masculine, Sun/thunder gods. During times of preservation, each Muse offered the gift of their specific talents i.e., music, art, science and literature. However, during periods of cyclic renewal, one would manifest from among them (Sibyls) to become the prophetic voice of the Divine African Mother (Mami).

ORIGIN OF THE NAME "*SIBYL*"

The name "*Sibyl*" is of mixed origins. It is the sacred initiatory title that the ancient Africans called the prophetess/priestesses of the Mami Watas. According to some, it is derived from the black *Ethiopian/Cushites* known as the *Phrygians* (natives of Mycenae). Their name of endearment for *Mami* was "*Cybele*," (*Cybella/Cybylle/Kybele*), *"Queen of Heaven; Mother of the Gods."*[10] Some scholars believe that "*Sibyl*" is a Greek corruption of two words, *Sioi,* meaning *"god,"* and "*bule,*" meaning *"to counsel*". Both words are derived from their Afro-Aeolitic dialect of ancient Mycenea. Combined, it reads as "*Siobule,*" which phonetically evolved into the English "*Sibyl.*"

Additionally, Webster's dictionary defines a *Sibyl* as "*a female prophet,*" or *"a woman able to utter the oracles and prophecies of a god; or a woman who can foretell the future."* Conversely, under the bitter Hebrew patriarchs, the Sibyls are condemned in their Bible, as *"Behalath-Ob"*, meaning *"evil serpent/spirit,"* or *"mistress of the Python."* However, when all is said and done, the Sibyls refer to themselves as "*Sisters of Isis,* and sometimes [*prophetesses*] of *the black Di-ana"*[11]

THE HOLY SIBYLLINE ORACLES

The Sibylline Oracles are a series of divine prophecies given over a span of more than three thousand years, that contain accurate global predictions, and chronicle the rise and fall of great empires and the destinies and fate of important heads of states, village kingdoms, their leaders and their nations.

These cycles usually entailed prophesying the coming of a "*holy one*." This "holy one" was not an apocalyptic "*savior*" sent to "*save*" all humankind, but rather the usual savior sun/thunder deities whose life was offered as a human sacrifice to purify the negative accumulation of karma, and announce the new groom of the Divine Mother. The idea of a "sole savior" probably began with the killing of the first *Annuki (fish* deity) sent to liberate and redirect the dangerously aggressive masculine tendencies of the patriarchal rebellions always threatening to destabilize the natural, social and political order of matriarchal society. Usually, the traditional target of their masculine aggression was aimed at overthrowing the divine matriarchies and their much coveted political and economic position established by the God/dess, which they maintained as the central seat of sacerdotal and secular power in the world.

These necessary cycles of human destruction and rebuilding (regeneration), traditionally entailed the customary sacrificial (savior/scapegoat) "*death and resurrection*" ceremonies. The ritual purgations, purifications, corrections of personal and societal errors (in violation of taboos) and the relief and justice for the suffering masses.[12] These Sibyls prophetic utterances were written down by scribe priests and priestesses, many complied in each individual Omphaé and temple shrine across the world.

For example, during the coming of one future cycle, it was Plato who later revealed the secret that at Delphi, there was an ancient secret prophecy concerning the birth of a son of Apollo (Osiris/Horus) who was to be the one to restore the reign of "*justice and virtue on earth.*" Godfrey Higgins claims that these Sibyl prophecies were actually referring to either the black *Buddha,* or black "*Cresna/Krishna*", both who were actually born on the holy Grecian island of *Dodona.*[13]

At Delphi, it was "*Cybele*" later known as Themis/ Artemis, Black-Di-ana." These Sibyls when seized by the spirit, would fall into possession, causing them to "*thrash about the ground," uttering messages from the gods.*[14] More often, it was a divine ancestor, expressing her/his unhappiness with those who were in violation of divine law.

She'd utter warnings and admonitions to the villages, cities and ancient kingdoms and their leaders; prophesying their doom, or fulfilling their hopes and restoring lost glory. She'd right moral wrongs and punish offenders of the divine law. She'd heal the sick call-up the dead, and restore dignity and strength to weak.

These prophecies were consistent and similar with those uttered by the chief Sibyl priestesses of the major Omphaé shrines scattered all across the ancient Mediterranean world. After realizing their intrinsic value, it was these prophecies that were later competitively seized and collated by the Roman Papals and Levitical Jews during their religio-political wars. They were compiled, doctored and plagiarized by them as they exist today in what has become known as the "*The Sibylline Oracles.*"[15]

THE SACERDOTAL MATRIARCH OF THE SIBYLS

By the Eleventh century C.E., Turkish monk and world historian, Cedrinus, claimed that the *Queen of Sheba* was a Sibyl. Prior to Egypt's dynastic period, the civil and religious culture of these matriarchal Sibs flourished in the Mediterranean world for more than 6,000 years[16]

For centuries, the Grecian islands at *Delos, Dodona, Delphi* and the temple of Mami in Libya, were the ecclesiastical and moral hub of religious, social and international political activity. As the first established, sacerdotal, African matriarchs, the Sibyls cultural and religious impact was arguably the most profound, on ancient civilization than history has ever revealed or care to admit. From Mesopotamia, to Libya, Mizarim (Kemet/Egypt), Ionia, Minoa, Peloponnese (Turkey) and Mycenae (Greece) and later Rome, the Sibyls were the primary, divine Vatican and absolute moral authority.

Just as their Divine African Mother, *Mami-Isis* served as the first universal, sacerdotal symbol of the "Divine Celestial and Terrestrial African Ancestress", Her worship as the manifestation of the *logos* was continued in Asia Minor (Cushitic Mitanni Empire) and in Minoa and Mycenae (Aegean Islands). Archeological pottery shards date the black descendants of the Libyan, *Garamantes* (present day *Ewe/Alladas/Ga-Adangbe*) and other African clans who had settled into Babylon and elsewhere, before the Flood, to have arrived in Minoa (Ionia) as early as 4000 B.C.E [17]

In Minoa and Mycenae, later renamed "*Greece*", it was under the theocratic governance of the Sibyls, as Queen Mothers, that African matriarchal culture reached its "golden age" of achievement in *medicine, religion, astronomy, philosophy, law, architecture, music, art* and social sophistication.

Under this same matriarchal sacerdotal order an era of high diplomacy, mutual cooperation and peace ensured.

The Sibyl clans were furhter divided into Sibs, similar to extended family villages. As "*Sibs*" they were the queen mothers and priestesses of their individual family totems and ancestral deities. "*Sibs*,"[18] are an extension of the per-historic, African matriarchal custom of (usually) three major matrilineal clans joining their tutelary and ancestral deities together, forming loose confederations, amounting to "one clan unit". Individuals initiated into the mysteries were "reborn" as a "*Sibyl*" or "*Pythias*" the same way that they are "reborn" as "*Mamaissii,*" or "*Amengansie*" in the Mami Wata Vodoun, within their respective Sib (Ewe, Fon, Mina, Anlo i.e.,). However, within the tradition, they may be simply addressed as "*Ma, Nana or Mama.*"

Fig 5: 400 B.C.E. red clay vessel of black, Minoan priestess in corn-rolled hair, during Greek colonization. The entire cultural, religious, economic and political substratum of what came to be credited as "*Greek culture,*" was actually that of these black matriarchs who fled the patriarchal takeovers in Libya, Egypt, and Ethiopia © Sadigh Gallery

Together, they constructed massive temples dedicated to Mami and all of her off-spring (deities) whose authoritative influence and divine power extended to all four corners of the known world. It was in those sacred temples that the Sibyls would offer their divine wisdom, healing and prophetic counsel. As *Avatars, Muses, Vestals* and Saints of the Mami Watas, all divine power later attributed to the most highest male god and prophets, was first accomplished by the priest/esshoods, headed by these holy, African queen mothers. All nations, even up until to the Roman period, depended on the prophesy, advice and divine knowledge of these African priestesses, uttering the words of their African deities.

The powerful confederations of city states collectively known as the *Minoan* and *Mycenaean* culture, consisted of *Ionia, Libyan Crete*, (also known as *Keftiu* by Egyptians), *Argos, Arcadia, Ephesus, Cythera, Corinth, Thessaly, Samothrace, Lydia, Lesvos, Phrygia, Mysia, Lycia, Rhodes, Peloponnese* (now Turkey) and many others. It was there where black matriarchy reigned supreme under the watchful guidance of the Divine African Mothers, who were defended by an Amazonian garrison. These sites were spiritually and culturally enriched havens where commerce, poetry, music, theater, architecture, philosophy, and astronomy flourished. An ancient region later invaded and inhabited by the Greeks, Persians and Turks (who arrived some 2500 years later) would be exclusively credited with developing these civilizations. [19]

However, both Briffault and Herodotus asserts their early African matriarchal roots and tell us that:

"... the earliest temples of Delphi was a thatched hut. In Lydia, the dwelling-houses ... were mostly built of reed and mud. There can be little doubt that, like the African kraals which they resembled, they were built by [African] women." [20]

Diner further informs us that as these ancient black matriarchies began to prosper, they built grand civilizations that *"became the envy of the known world."* We are told that *"the girls and boys went to school together and learned geometry, grammar and even square roots and that anyone operating a business had to keep books".* [21]

Diner further reports that:

The capitol of Lydia became the Paris of Asia Minor, greater than Greece. One imported the most
elegant of cloth, perfumes, and the fine, high-heeled shoes so much in demand in Sappho's [poetry]
circles " . . . it was also a male beauty center, featuring such attractions as permanents, gold jewelry,
manicuring and dental cures . . . [and] whoever thought that the Chaldean [Rehki diviners] were too
expensive has his horoscope prepared by the Lycian ladies.[22]

In Asia Minor, (now Turkey), the science of medicine had
its origins and the first great temple to the African ancestral python
"*Asclepias*" was built. Moreover, it was on these black, matriarchal
islands that *Hippocrates* learn to conduct the first scientific
investigations of anatomy and disease.

Later, the sons of Rome flocked to learn medicine at Her
schools and distinguished African "*physicians tended to their
Emperors, consuls and military commanders.*" We further learn
that the languages of both Greek and Latin, as well as their tonal
musical scales are derived directly from the Afro-[Phonecian]
Aeolian and *Phyrgian* dialects of these African and Elamite
matriarchal groups.[23]

The pre-Grecian Island of Rhodes, named after its original
black inhabitants, was originally known as *Pelasgia*, meaning
"*sailors*" or the "*Daughters of the Sea.*" They were said to have
"*furnished literature and history with inexhaustible material and
rendered invaluable services to the fine arts and exact science and
applied mechanics. . . [and] a code of maritime legislation was
formulated . . . which has formed the basis of all subsequent
studies on th[e] subject*".[24]

However, although Rhodes was said to have maintained a
hundred images of the Sun God, "*Apollo,*" and one to *Mami*, whom
they knew as "*Laocoon,*" with her serpents", it was the Grecian
island of

Delos, that housed the Vatican of the African Goddess and Her consort Gods. Hailed as one of the "*Seven Wonders of the World*", these sacred temples were maintained by the Sibyls and a contingent of vestal "virgin" priestesses and eunuchs.

These African deities never walked in the flesh. For more than one thousand years, the sacred island was free from war, crime and invasions; thus, borders were never necessary. Here is where *Ar-Themis* (Artemis, later "*Black-Di-nana*") was said to have been born next to the Sacred Lake, along with *Isis*, *Anubis* and *Serpais*. More divinities were added as the African and Elamite (Tamil) populations increased.[25]

The place was covered with holy temples and colossal marble statues of the deities. There were clubs, markets and palaces. White robe processions in honor of some deity were always in session. According to Horton they maintained a system of bartering in goods and their trade routes to Palestine, Egypt, Lybia, Athens, Corinth, Crete, Peloponnese (Turkey) and others, "*enumerated a list of which would make a poem.*"[26]

Horton further tells us that: One came to Delos as pilgrim and merchant . . . the place swarmed with bartering humanity. Commerce and religion were interfused, or connected like Siamese twins, if one died, the other gave-up the ghost.[27]

Their temples were deemed so holy, that one could only live, but never be born, die or buried on the island. Sacrifices were also forbidden. Any sacrifices had to be performed on the neighboring islands. If either birth or death was imminent, one was transported to another island.[28]

Later, when the patriarchal Persians (Aryans/Iranians) had their turn at invading, pillaging and destroying all of the other island temples and slaughtering its inhabitants, when they arrived at Delos, they were so in awe, that they left it untouched.[29]

We are further told that these African and Elamite matriarchal confederations would come together at the main oracular temple in Ephesus (built by their Amazons), to worship the "*Queen of Heaven*," who was known in their own tongue by many names. The most popular being *Ar-Themis, Cybele, Ceres, Demeter, Atargatis* and *"Dione--* and just as the Helen of Troy, they too were all black.[30] It was at the Ionian island of *Cythera* (*Cergio*) where black *Aphrodite* first rode upon the foam of a great wave and demanded that a temple be built to her. Soon many more gods would follow.

The African Gods/desses heading these divine pantheons *Isis/Asaase/ Inanna/ Ashtoreth/ Atagatis/ Cybelle/Demeter/ Hathor/Black-Di-ana* etc.,. were the major water deities who were known by many names in the theology of the Mami Wata tradition: They are descended from the original *logos*, which is known in Kemet (Egypt) as "*Isis*." *Isis* is a divine concept which embodies this logos as "*divine wisdom*."[31]

As the first African and Ancestress, she is also recognized as the first divine queen, possessed of the full power of Mami. She herself was not God, but rather its divine wisdom [*Sededé,/Maat/logos*] first divine "crowned" manifestation in human form, whose rites are known as "*Mami Wata*." Her name, just as that of *Osiris* and *Horus* became synonymous with the *Netjer* and the names *"Isis*, "*Sibyl*", "*Mamaissii*," and others are particularly commensurate with one initiated as a "*serpent water priestess*".

BLACK AMAZONS: IN DEFENSE OF *MOTHER-RIGHT*

BLACK AMAZONS: IN DEFENSE OF *MOTHER-RIGHT*

Fig 6: Libyan Amazonian queen *Penthesilea,* who led her army of warriors against the Greeks during the Trojan war. She was eventually killed by Achilles, who allegedly found her beauty so irresistible, that he sexually seduced her dead body.

Often referred to in Western history as *mythological* figures, or as *Europeans,* the ancient black Amazon (*Ama* = *mother*; *zon* = Sun, *"mother of the Sun people")* were historic, and they were African. The oldest militia were probably the *Ethiopians, Egypto-Libyans, Scythians* and the ancient *Colchians* of Colchis, in what is now southern Russia. However, large garrisons of the Amazons were scattered all throughout the ancient world, including in the *Caucasus, Albania, Athens, India, Armenia, Boeotia,* (central Greece) *Atlantis. Asia,* and even in North America. The Amazons were known under many names, i.e, *Azones, Alazones, Syri, Assyrii, Chaldei, Mauri, Chalybes* etc. They were the original *"shock-troops,"* fighting in defense of the ancient temples, and kingdoms of the black matriarchs (*mother-right*) which dominated the ancient world. It was the black Amazons who were the first to domestic and to ride chariots and horses when the Greeks did not.
They were the first to employ calvary, and their superior weaponry was made of iron, when the Greeks were still using bronze.

Fig 7: Greek vase of ancestral, totemic ritual mask of black, Libyan Amazon who settled in ancient Crete and Athens more than 3,000 years before the Greeks. The mask represented the powerful talismaic spirit of their founding ancestress, known by many names including *Mudesa, Stheino, and Euryale* (Walker, p. 349). They were the first initiates of the African, *huntress, Mami* goddess, know as *Athena, Minerva*, and *Ar-themis* Known as the *"Mask of Gorgon,"* it was worn only by the queen Amazon mothers/generals. It was the main source of spiritual power, physical strength and maternal wisdom; and when worn during battle or ceremonial ritual, it evoked paralyzing fear into the hearts of the Greek and Spartan soldiers. It would literally freeze them to death in their tracks, which is where the myth *"turning men to pillars of stone"* originated. Historians tried to dismiss the black color of these ancient Greek vase depictions as *"black laquer art,"* but history has proved that the color is based on accurate accounts of the Amazons as black, and African.

As initiated priestesses of the triple-headed, black, warrior/hunter/fertility Mami goddess, *Athena/Minerva Ar-themis,* their extraordinary knowledge of herbs, and use of magic and ceremonial ritual to achieve political and military objectives was unparallel.

The Greeks bitterly referred to them as *"man-murdering, man-hating, flesh devouring, and war lustful,* etc," and are directly responsible for many of the lies and myths circulating as "history" about them today. Far from being a hostile contingent of disaffected *"men haters,"* Higgins reports that these black Amazons were actually the *"original followers of the male and female principles,"* (vol 1. p. 507), and fought to maintain the balance of both, rather than the exclusive rule of patriarchy being advocated by the sun priests of Amon.

The Amazons were also the actual builders of the ancient temples of *Astarte, Ar-themis, Minerva Black Di-Ana, Demeter* etc.,. And founded and named all of the city and provinces in which they settled and erected their temples.

The Greeks who feared and hated the black Amazons, fought voracious battles against them. One of their most famous battles with these fearless women warriors, was in *Attica,* in ancient Athens which ended in a truce.

The Greeks who feared and hated the black Amazons, fought voracious battles against them. One of their most famous battles with these fearless women warriors, was in *Attica*, in ancient Athens which ended in a truce.

The commander of the Amazons in Attica was black Egyptian queen, *Eumolphus*, who ordered that sacrifices be made to their ancestral (Manes) deities by the Athenians. (vol. p. 506). A stone pillar exist today in the *Amazoneum*, erected to signify this truce, because the Greeks could not defeat them.   Lederer reports that the Greek's willingness to go to battle against these black Amazons was *"used. . . as a measure of [their] courage,"* and that they, in facing the Amazons, *"faced not only their biological aversion against fighting with women, but also their own castration anxiety,"* (pg. 104).

7 b: Bronze plate of Amazon. It was the black Amazons who were the first to domestic and to ride chariots and horses. They were the first to employ calvary, and their superior weaponry was made from iron.

The black Amazons were also the original *megalith, Cyclopes and Stonehenge* builders, and are credited with founding and building many of the ancient *Ionian* and *Aegean* island cities now credited to the Greeks.   They were the actual builders of the ancient, so-called *"biblical"* city of *Ephesus, Corinth,* and others. They also named all of these sacred cities including *Euphesus,* which means *"Moon city,"* which acted as their chief center of operations.   Euphesus was eventually destroyed and rebuilt seven times. The first in 1490 B.C.E., destroyed by the Amazons themselves, rather than succumb to the hostile take-over of their temples by Egyptian, priest and military leader *Sesostris* (Falkener, p. 165).

It was also *at Ephesus* and Corinth where the converted, jew turned Christian "Paul" was made a "saint" by the Roman Church, for helping to orchestrate the destruction of much of the ancient black matriarchal temples of black Di-Ana, and forcing Christianity upon its citizenry.   As patriarchy held sway around the world, the foreign invaders, i.e., Assyrians, Greeks, Turks, Roman and others, on many occasions would often join forces with the Amazon's African patriarchal enemies in order

Fig 7c: Yahi, (now deceased), one of the last remaining Amazons in West Africa. Far from being localized to only ancient Dahomey by Western historians, the black Amazons, initiates of the African Mami deity *Athena/Ar-themis/Ephesia (Black Di-Ana)*, were the first organized battalion of female warriors in the world. They were a major militaristic contingency throughout all of ancient Africa, in defense of their matriarchies. Historically, they were called "Zon, Zoan, On, etc.," and a host of other names. They conquered lands and founded cities and built extraordinary temples, naming them after themselves or after their queen mother or goddess. Heliopolis in northern Egypt was originally called *Zoan*. Cities in *Thrace, Armenia, Cappadocia* (ancient Turkey), in the *Caucasus, Albania, Athens, Attica* and elsewhere throughout the ancient world, were founded and named after these fearless black warriors.

to defeat them. The African patriarchs having superior knowledge of their ritual magic, therefore knew how to fight against them successfully. In fact, many of the epic tales recounting the greatness of black heros such as Hercules, *Theseus* and others, was due to them being able to defeat the Amazonian queens by stealing their ritual girdle, talismans, thunder axes, etc., thereby defeating the source of their enormous military might. Once conquered and destroyed, these men were hailed as "heros." Such was the case when *Theseus* killed the sacred *Minotaur* of the queen goddess, and when Hercules stole the sacred ancestral girdle of Amazonian queen *Hippolyte*, weakening her, and then slaughtering her entire army.

Overtime, the Amazons were eventually defeated world-wide, and erased from the annals of world history, or relegated to "Greek *mythology*," their African identity and great history concealed. However, centuries later, in a daring act by West African Dahomean, *King* Agadja *(1708-1732)*, a garrison of the Amazons were restored. An unprecedented move in which they served a patriarchal ruler rather than their queen mothers. The entire history of the black Amazons and the immense role they played in developing African spiritual history, culture and military expansion throughout the ancient world is beyond the scope of this book, and could easily take volumes. Their story is yet to be completely told.

HISTORY OF BLACK MATRIARCHS CONCEALED IN EURO-BIBLICAL REVISIONISTS HISTORY

If African-American Christian women knew the untold history behind many of the biblical locations of which they offer their glory, they would be horrified to learn that they were lending a glorious praise to locations where their ancient mothers were murdered, and persecuted, and their holy temples seized and converted into "Christian churches"; and where their African deities were demonized and their veneration and worship ultimately destroyed. Unraveling the mental shackles of western religious brainwashing affected by colonialism and slavery, is one of the few areas many in the diaspora ever dare challenge.

Few realize that even before the dawn of African patriarchy, in the oldest story of Genesis, it was Mami-Isis who originally gave birth to the sky, earth and to the water divinities. These mythos would later be changed crediting these events to "*Osiris*" and "Amon," and then exported into their Egyptian colonies where their names would be honored in the indigenous vernacular as "*Zeus, Apollo and Dionsysus*". The Sibyls who were from wealthy families were as a rule, the most educated, cultured and talented amongst their class. However, the most prophetically powerful and ritually skillful Sibyls could be either literate or not able to read or write.

The Spirit delighted in those who came from poor and humble backgrounds, just as much as those from the privileged class. If they were initiated and raised in the temples, they possessed their own sacred language and other sacrosanct customs. In ancient Sumer, this language was called, "*emesal*" for the priestesses and "*emegir*" for the order of male priests. In the

Mami Wata Vodoun, depending on the dialect, this sacred language is known as "*vodogbe*."

Nonetheless, it was these Sibyls, joined with what evolved into the Chaldean order of black, male astronomers/diviners/augurs, known as "Rekhi" in ancient Egypt, flanked by a militia of Amazons, who were the primary defenders of "Mother-right." It was their divine duty to establish, defend and maintain the, predominance of the, matriarchal kingdoms and religious temples, being erected throughout the ancient world.

There, in white robed ceremonial processions, they would conduct elaborate richly ornate and lavish fetes whose synergistic blends of traditional ritual and musical themes, seemed to span the cultural taste of the entire continent of Africa and southern India. "Calling down the gods" and possessions were their primary goal; each fete executed with expert

Fig8: 400 C.E. mural depicting Afro-Chaldean builders forced to construct the hypogeum of "Christian" martyr Trebius Justus. Because they were all black, the Greeks rightfully made no distinction between the ancient Chaldeans, Egyptians, Canaanites, and the Phoenicians.[32] They along with the Amazons were an order of highly talented temple, cyclopean stone builders and polishers, traders, and master diviner priests. It is they, and not the Greeks or Romans who are the original builders of the pillars and monumental temples of the ancient African god/desses. The U.S. White House and other structures take their design from these talented masons.

proficiency and grace. Higgins asserts that these confederations consisted of twelve tribes and that *Herodotus* and referred to them as "*the self-governing peoples*" because they were the first to form a democracy.

Their advanced style of government would be known in modern times as the *"Lycian Confederacy,"* and centuries later in the New World, became the inspiration for Alexander Hamilton, John Jay and James Madison to praise them as an *"excellent Confederate Republic."*

In an ironic twist of historical events, in the formation of America's democracy, though the African themselves were enslaved, they employed this matriarchal, African model of government as the "perfect model of democracy" when writing the Declaration of Independence."[33.]

These African matriarchs were also the first to institute gold coinage, and to build store front shops. Modeling after the *Grand Lodge of Luxor*, ancient Egypt's great library, (later renamed renamed *"Alexander"*) the matriarchs too had built one of the first libraries for developing intellectuals and students of the mystery schools.[34]

Bachofen tell us that:

... They [the black matriarchs] bore within themselves the law pervading all matter. Justice speaks out of their mouths without self-consciousness and with certainty in the manner of conscience. They are wise by nature, prophetesses proclaiming *Fate, Sibyl,* or *Themis*. Therefore women were considered inviolable bearers of jurisprudence and sources of prophecy.[35]

Similarly, Diner states that:

Everything in circulation among our [European] astrologists and other 'prophetesses' under the name of '*The Egyptian Dream Book*', was copied from the work of [Lycian priest] *Artemidoros* [priest of *Mami Arthemis*] of Daldis, who worked out his interpretation of some three thousand dreams in five volumes during the second century B.C.E

Additionally, there was for more than two thousand years, the Karayounani (black Ionian) inhabitants of ancient Thessaly. *"Thessaly"* meaning *"the sea or moon* people" is a mountainous region in central Greece.

The prefix "*Kara*", was coined by the later invading Turks, meaning "*black*," and the suffix "*younani*' was added by the later invading Persians, meaning "*Ionian.*" Thessaly was a thriving center of Afro-esoteric learning, numberous holy temples, grand festive rituals and rich culture. [36]

Fig 9: 450 C.E. catacomb of persecuted martyr "*Petronilla*" showing a Sibyl priestess standing next to a sacred omphaé, with serpent and what probably is her prophecies in the book above it. Most of the real identity of the scenes on the Roman catacombs were either destroyed or later concealed and credited to "*Christian*" martyrs by present day historians, who are ignorant of the sacred symbolism of the Mami Wata priestshoods.

Centuries later, Thessaly too would be destroyed, and renowned famed as the ancient location where the "biblical" Paul's proselytizers were chased out and killed for insulting the African deities and attempting to force its inhabitants to accept an alien god and theology (see *Thessalonians* I, II). It is here also where Paul first tested the (now badly corrupted Euro-Christianized) Sibyl prophecies against her own people, knowing that they would obey her words.

Thessaly, along with all of the surrounding Afro-Indian inhabited islands where Papal officials determined to discredit and destroy all vestiges of the true Afro-esoteric traditions of the Sibyl prophecies from which they heavily borrowed, would later be branded by Paul and his proselytes, as the notorious home of "*evil, heathens, witches, talismans and [makers of] love-philters.*" [37]

During the Pharaonic era, the Pharaohs selected their wives from amongst the Sibyl clans, which was how they [Pharaohs] could claim authority through divine descent. In the prophetic *Book of Kings*, (whose authorship is allegedly "unknown") King Solomon, already a priest of the Mami divinity *"Ashtoreth,"* *(Astarte)* was later accused of marrying "many other girls besides the Egyptian princess . . . *who came from nations where idols were worshiped . . . Amon, Edom, Sidon and from the Hitties.*" (Kings 1, 11:1-6).

All of these historic locations were where the Sibyls maintained major oracular Mami shrines. Important to note is that the ancient depiction of the "ochre" colored wives of the Pharaoh was not a racial designation, but an ancient custom (still practiced in present day Togo and Benin). In this practice an African who is of another clan is designated by a different hue or the path of the deity from which they descend, is esoterically denoted by the color characteristic. This ritual was not originally employed to denote "race." for example, ochre (usually symbolizing motherblood), was often employed to designate the lineages from the ancient Canaanite matrilineal Sibs.

Prophetic Style of Siblys

The Sibyls prophetic messages were heard during ritual ceremonies of ecstatic (trance) possessions, or they were magically induced through sacred herbal blends, and other divinatory means. Oftentimes, they were fully focused as the deity manifested in their heads, while they (or someone else) wrote their utterances down on laurel or palm leaves. Several Greek and Roman historians recount how the Sibyl's poetic utterances were written down by scribe priestesses, as they lay "*thrown about the ground in ecstatic trance* [possession]." Lewis tells us that they were "mounted by the thunder god "Apollo", whose spirit rode on the nape of their (the Sibyl's) neck."[38]

Though Roman Church revisionists favored the latter as being more "pure," this is an arrogant distortion of the sacro-spiritual mysteries of which they and the world have never been privy. Oftentimes, it was in divination sessions within the confines of their own shrines, aided by scribes who would write down their utterances. All these methods are still in extant within contemporary Yeveh Mami Wata Vodoun, and other Afro-spiritual traditions.

Fig 10: 199-217 C.E. scene from a catacomb of the Hebrew prophet "Jo-nah" with Sibyl and priest making sacrifice.

The Divine African Mother, as Isis, Mami, Arthemis et.al., the serpent divinity, would overtake them and begin to utter through them. Depending on the location and ancestral (Sib) lineage, all of the above holy names were merely esoteric designations meaning "*Wisdom*" or "*I proceed from myself*". Sometimes, she (the divine Spirit) would call herself "*Isis*", sometimes, "[black] Di-ana" and sometimes *Minerva, Athena or Mami.*"[39]

The Sibyls Influence in Ancient Rome

Although there were other competing patriarchal gnostic sects such as the *Teutonics,* the Galla/ Ethiopian Durids, Buddhists, Mithras Manichaens, and the Muslims, the Roman Empire depended almost exclusively on the Sibyl prophecies, and their magical ministrations. The Sibyls along with their college of African diviners (augury), were the Roman Empire's main source of divine and ethical guidance.

Fig 11: Ancient stelae of a Sibyl from Carthage advertising her lineage and probably her spiritual services. On top is the "*Celestial Hand*" of the Divine African Mother, whom in this stelae is *Astarte-Tanit*. Below, is the holy Omphaé, crowned with the solar disk, encircled by the sacred rays (or twin serpents). The "*black doves*," (holy spirit) represent the antiquity and lineage of the Omphaé. Just as in the tradition of the ancient Chaldeans, the Celestial [left] Hand was originally the emblem of the Mami Goddess, Ninhursag displayed on the Babylonian pyramid at Borsippa. Under African patriarchy, it was later changed to the right-hand of the Sun deity Amon/Anu, and renamed "*The Temple of the Right Hand*," or the "*Hand of Anu.*" However, it was the nurturing and magical [left] hand of the African Mother, that led to hand emblems being placed atop homes from Morocco, Libya, to Palestine, to ward of evil. The Christians soon appropriated this symbol made famous as the "Hand of God." In the Mami Wata Vodoun, the left hand is still recognized as the most powerful.

monopolize the Sibyl's prophetic books exclusively for themselves.[40] The most important being those prophecies referencing their (Rome's) own eventual destruction. Important strategic information that they wanted desperately to conceal from their military enemies.

This was especially true during Rome's territorial battles with the Greek *Cleopatra* and her husband/brother *Antony*, who now ruled Egypt.

The Roman Emperor, Augustus Caesar (Octavian), on many occasions, sought consultation with the Sibyl, *Tiburtina* (in Cumae, Italy), but she would categorically refuse him. She did this because he had just declared himself "Caesar", (meaning "*Lord or God*") of all of Rome and demanded to be addressed as such. This, no Sibyl could do. However, under much pressure, Tiburtina was forced to see him. In 27-30 B.C.E the Roman Emperor, finally arrive for a divination and just as the Spirit was taking possession of her, Mami descended, and appeared before him.

Shocked and frightened at what was to transpire next, the "great Caesar" learned quickly who was the true "*Lord.*" The emperor was alleged to have exclaimed that he "*saw the heavens rent open and she [African Mami-Isis] sitting on an altar . . . holding a child in her arms.*" Amazed and in dumb-struck awe, the emperor quickly "*prostrated himself onto the ground*" before them, offering "*thanks and praises to God.*" From that moment onward, Augustus never demanded to be addressed as "God or Lord," by the African clergy again.

As a blessing for his humility, Mami promised the great Caesar victory over his number one arch enemy, the great, black Carthaginian general, *Hannibal,* as long as he promised not to invade and to destroy all of Carthage. Particularly, the great temple of Tanit. She also made him promise to install a shrine consecrated to her, and to not suppress her worship by any of her people in the Roman colonies. The emperor immediately agreed to erect a temple in Rome where Mami would be venerated by all (including "white") Romans. [41]

After Rome's military success, in chasing Hannibal and his army out of Rome, the Caesar kept his promise to the Divine African Mother. On April 4, 204 B.C.E amongst great pomp and celebration replete with plenty of miracles along the journey, the statue "*Ara Coeli,*" meaning *Altar of Heaven,* embodied in the sacred, black *Pessinuncian stone,* was installed. She was placed in the temple next to the black goddess "*Nike/Victory*" located on the famous Palatine Hill.

That spring, Rome experienced a bumper harvest and Hannibal fled Italy back to North Africa. It was also no coincidence that the years immediately following the installation of the Divine African Mother became known as the "*Augustan Age.*" An era considered one of the most "*illustrious periods in Latin history.*" It was during this period (29 B.C.E - 18 C.E.) when Latin culture was marked by "*civil peace and prosperity,*" and reached it highest literary and poetic expressions," including Virgil's "*Georgics*" and the completion of the *Aeneid.*" [42]

Foreign Affairs and Miraculous Cures

Augustus was not the only notable figure who sought the expert advice and divine wisdom of the Sibyls. He was merely following the age old custom of African kings, military leaders, entrepreneurs, village chiefs and heads of states, who understood that if they wanted to be successful in their endeavors, it was prudent to seek the counsel of a local Sibyl priestess.

In one account, Alexander *the Great*, was initially refused a divination by the Sibyl priestess, until she was literally "dragged towards the tripos," by one of the overseers priest of Amon who forced her to perform a divination for him. That is when she is said to have uttered her famous words to *the Great* Alexander, *"my son thou art invincible."*[43]

Similarly, Croesus, the Phrygian [black] King of Lydia, before he finalized his declaration of war against the Persians, visited all of the Sibyl shrines in Greece, including sending ambassadors all the way to the shrine of *Amon* in Libya to seek the consult of the wise Sibyls. So unimpeachable and esteemed was the wisdom of these African mother priestesses, that heads of states when instituting new laws would even imply that their laws were sanctioned by the Sibyls because they knew the people would promptly comply.[44]

Seeking advice in matters of foreign affairs was not all these black prophetess' could claim as legendary. Their oracles were credited with divine miracles just as the black *Bakides* (male prophets of the ancestral *Dionysus*). The Sibyl prophecies were the first to be universally written into scriptural versus and employed as protective amulets, because they were believed to ward off evil. These potent versus were often consulted as divine omens, and the necessary sacrifices were offered to prevent death, sickness, poverty and natural disasters.

For example, such was the case when many took heed to the Sibyl warnings of a massive earthquake which resulted in the death of thousands, leaving an outbreak of pestilence in its wake. Or, the account of the raining down of thunder stones where propitiation to the pythonian thunder god was prescribed by the Sibyls. It was also the Sibylline oracles that prescribed the necessary sacrifices to the priests/ess to appease all of the divinities in the temples.[45]

It was also these African matriarchies under the auspices of the Sibyls who were the civilizing authority in which all new waves of foreign immigrants, no matter how barbarous, would be gradually subdued and systematically integrated into the main society. However, no matter how "civilized" or culturally assimilated, none of these groups were ever allowed knowledge of the mysteries, which remained the exclusive domain of the African priestesshood. Even long after their colonization by the barbarous Dorians [Greeks], though they (the Greeks) claimed to be "*Sons of [the non-Egyptian] Heracles,*" these primitive groups had not yet been tamed and assimilated as the earlier wave of *Libyans, Aeolians* and *Ionian* immigrants. Thus, it was forbidden for them to even enter into the sacred chambers of the Sibyls, whom these earlier Greeks often worshiped as god/desses. In one account, Herodotus tells us of an exchange between the Sibyl high priestess, *Herophile* and a Dorian [Greek] invader, during their violent seize of Athens. He recounts that:

. . . when he [a Greek] first went up into the citadel, meaning to seize it, just as he was entering the sanctuary of the goddess, in order to question her, the priestess arose from her throne, before he had passed the doors, and said- 'Stranger from Lacedaemon, depart hence, and presume not to enter the holy place- it is not lawful for a Dorian to set foot there[!][46]

On another occasion, Aeneas, the Pelasgian, Trojan war hero and initiate into the tradition of the black-Venus, reported his experience after visiting for a divination at the famous Sibyl cave of *Apollo*, at Cumae (Rome). He recounts that:

There is on the Enbaum Coast a vast Cave cut out of the Rock, into which opens a hundred mouths, whence do proceed as many voices; which are the answers of the Sibyl. [He came] to the entrance when the Prophetess said, "Tis time to pray for revelations: The Divinity, the Divinity is present." As she spake the words, at the very entrance her countenance, and color changed, and her hair was disordered; her breast heaved, and her violent passions swelled her: she seemed bigger than ordinary, and her voice appeared to be different from that of Mortals upon this her immediate seizure by the Divinity.[47]

The author   assures us that what Aeneas reported actually transpired. He further tells us that:

> . . . the entire coast of which is now called Italy was devoted to that [African] God, and called *Saturnia* by the inhabitants. That Aeneas and the Trojans came to Italy, all the Roman authors assure us; and so do the Solemnities used in their Sacrifices   and Festivals, as also the Sibylline and Pythic Oracles; and many other indications there are of the same. [48]

"Saturnalia" was a major African and Tamil festive day to celebrate the safe journey of the Ancestors "*Io/Onnaes/*" from the flood.

Casting out Demons and Calling-up the Dead

The Sibyls were known to affect miraculous cures credited in today's Judeo-Christian tradition exclusively to Christ. However, it was originally the Sibyls prior to Christ who were hailed for giving sight to the blind, curing lameness, epileptics, deaf mutes and lepers. They were said to "*cast out demons*" and even to "*raise-up the dead.*" This last reference is probably meant to "call-up and materialize the spirit of a dead person." For example, the Cumean Sibyl, *Herophile* was famed for calling-up the spirit of the Apostle Samuel from the dead. This ancient ritual is still in practice today, performed by a sacred priesshood known as *Amenganssies* in the *Mami Wata Vodoun* traditions of West Africa.[49]

The Sibyls were also believed to be immortal and never to die. In one account, it was believed that their spirits:

> . . . "after [death] went into the Air, and became the Power of divination by Omens and Soothsayings: that her body was turned into Earth, and grew up . . . into Herbs" [50]

Life after death is a cosmogonic belief that has its counterpart in the Mami Wata Vodoun as the *Loko* tree and the Vodou *Azizas*.

The over embellished biblical lore recounting Christ sending a pantheon of "*demons*" into a "herd" of pigs" (Mark 5:1-20) was not an aberration from African sacrosanct divine priestly powers. Exorcizing malevolent spirits is a very common and customary purification African ritual, prescribed for most exorcisms or when the manifestational behavior of a deity demands the erection of an altar. One historic example of this occurred during the time of the Sibyls, when Athens had suffered a catastrophic plague, the Sibyls commanded that a purification rite be performed to appease the spirits. They did this by ceremoniously sending one black and one white sheep through the city, and wherever the sheep clasped an altar was to be erected.[51]

Oracles, Prophecies, and holy Maxims

As African civilizations established and maintained their military, political and cultural predominance in the ancient world, the Sibyls availed themselves to all the world's inhabitants. However,
they and their divinities were most comfortable within their own cultural milieu and the majority of their prophecies and daily ritual activities were originally localized and confined to the African city-states, towns and villages where their temples, clan totems, immediate and extended families resided. As long as these provinces were not violated or threatened with invasions, the deities as a rule remained apolitical and focused on the well-being and preservation of their own. However, the oracles and prophecies of the Sibyls were employed and trusted universally as the holy word of the Gods, and depended upon in all manner of life and sudden travails.

For examples, it was reported by Livy during the reign of Mark Antony that:

When, in the days of Mark Antony, soldiers were destroyed by storms, and owls and wolves invaded cities, when unexpected sun eclipses darkened the republic, when a thunderbolt damaged the scepter of Jupiter, and when animals brought forth creatures outside their species, the Sibylline oracles were made known with the result that some men became inspired and uttered prophecies.[52]

The popular phrase "*the lot or die has been cast*" is derived directly from the many forms of divination employed by the Sibyls/Pythias, in which either a dice or shells were thrown and read according to a list of characters written on a chart. The now widely used Christian custom of praying over unopened letters was already in practice for hundreds of years by some Sibyls, who actually divined and responded to their unopened letters accurately conveying the seekers prayers and inquires.[53]

Division in the Holy Empire: The Patriarchal Revolts

Before there were race and class wars, the first human factional wars were gender. The first groups to engage in such warfare were the Africans. The first level of power in which control was sought was spiritual, economic and political. Africans, possessing the highest levels of spiritual, magical and mystical power and knowledge, for centuries through their ambitious tutelary and clan gods, often competed and waged bitter spiritual warfare, of mythologic proportion against one another. These divine wars began as one between competing clan gods and soon escalated beyond what the gods had originally intended. The first apostasy (fall) against the Divine African Mother, appears to have taken place in ancient Egypt.

Historians of ancient Egypt when describing Egypt's rise as a global military power, often assume an amicable joining of upper and lower Egypt under King *Menes*, hailing this event as the greatest political achievement in Egyptian history. This monumental event the claim began the "golden age" of military conquest and global expansion, and the unchallenged rule of Egypt's patriarchal Pharaohs. And according to most, it established Egypt's enviable position as a legitimate world power. However, that is the view from history provided by the patriarchs. Upon closer examination in considering the historical evidence from the view of the matriarchs, indicates that this "amicable joining" might not have been such a crowning achievement in Egypt's history at all. But rather the opposite.

In spite of Egypt's patriarchal military might, the kings and pharaohs of Egypt still had to capitulate to the conquered and declining matriarchs for whom they still must claim their divine blood and spiritual inheritance. This inescapable fact, as well as her exclusive sacerdotal authority and political influence in the world, generated much jealously, envy and resentment towards them. So much that it is alleged that 1000 years later as matriarchal rule gave way to new waves of patriarchal revolts, the powerful priestshoods of Amon (Aum/ Amen) in *Khnum* and the clans of Horus boldly dared something never before imagined. They began invading and usurping the holy temples of these Divine African Mothers starting in Thebes.

They then invaded and usurped the major Sybil temples in Libya and Ethiopia. As a consequence, many of these matriarchal clans fled North and East Africa taking refuge on remote (now) Grecian island countries such and *Ionia*. Many in Thebes fled to the (now) Grecian *Argos* or settled into the ancient African Mittani kingdom territories in *Asia Minor* (Turkey). Many also fled to (now Grecian) *Mycenea* and re-built their temples; all continuing their service to Mami (Isis) known to them as "*Demeter*" and established sacred African societies such as the "*Thesmophorians*," and the "*Skirophorians*."[54] Finally, hundreds (if not thousands) of Sibyls and other priestesses opted instead to commit suicide by jumping into the Nile river rather than submit to patriarchal authority.[55]

Those temple priests of Amon who revolted against them slaughtered the ancestral python of the Sibyls. A deliberate act of divine warfare that centuries later, *Wegbaja,* the first king of Dahomey, is alleged to have committed in his takeover of sacerdotal power against the matriarchal clans in West Africa. After Amon's priests slaughtered the sacred python, they demanded that separate grand temples be built to *Apollo (Amon)* and Zeus (Horus) atop of them. These priests then proceeded to rearrange the cosmological pantheon placing themselves at the head. A new, patriarchal mythos was invented and the sacerdotal doves were replaced with the fiery eagles of Horus.

The Sibyls were then ordered to serve under Apollo and the thunder god Zeus (Horus), headed by male overseers. The priests then seized control over the Vestals (virgin priestesses) controlling all of their divine functions, especially that of prophecy and healing. According to Greek historian, *Pausania,* the Sibyls would often expressed their contempt against patriarchal aggression in sacred song and poetic verse.

In one famous song, recounting the historical truth about their genesis, Sibyl reminds these priests of her divine role in their very existence.

> For when the world was deluged with a flood
> Of waters, and one man of good repute
> Alone was left and in a wooden house
> Sailed o'er the waters with the beasts and birds,
> In order that the world might be refilled,
> I was his son's bride and was of his [Black] race
> To whom the first things happened and the last.
> Were all made known: and thus from mine own mouth
> Let all these truthful things remain declared.[56]

"*His sons bride*," is an allegorical reference, reminding the patriarchal masses that the divine kingships of which they proudly claim their legitimacy, is still wrought through the blood of the African mother. However, these veracious proclamations fell on deaf ears, and overtime, the matriarchies lost enormous political, economic and territorial ground.

Egypt's patriarchal wars began under Menes vying for total control of their ancient mother's empires across *Asia Minor, Libya, Troy* and *Italy* continued unabated. However, their competitors for these empires were not only other African patriarchs. Egypt had no shortage of enemies of whom they often waged a constant battle for control. Namely, the fiercely patriarchal *Levitical black Hebrews,* later followed by the *Dorian Greeks, and then the Assyrians, the Persians, the white Turks*, and finally, centuries later, the Romans.

In the holy temples seized by the priests of Amon, the *T'ache* (divine power) of the African matriarchs had long ago departed. Each temple was soon plagued by spiritual and political corruption, commercialization, internal power struggles, and sexual abuse. These crimes further aided to devalue and under mind the Sibyl's exclusive authority as the original and divine mouthpiece of the god/desses.

Over time, the oracular work (divinations) that traditionally only required one Sibyl to perform, now demanded the combined power of three.

Centuries later, after the invention of Christianity, "Bishop Eusebius" the so-called "*Father of Church History*," delighting in the decline of their most fiercest competitor, took advantage of this in advancing the Roman Papal's agenda against African spiritual predominance in the world. He propagandized and attributed the gradual collapse of the African matriarchies to *"Christ who exorcize all demons, including the . . . [Sibyl] oracles."*[66]

Although these unfortunate events began the decline of African matriarchal political power, it did not remove them entirely from their seat of sacerdotal power; in spite of the patriarchal takeover of their temples. The deity to whom these Sibyls were the mouth piece was still "*Mami*," who was worshiped under the many appellations of Isis (a title meaning "logos/wisdom"); and the fire/thunder spirit of the ancestral father python originally manifested by Horus, who became known under many names including *Asclepius, Dionysus, Attis, Zeus, Apollo,* etc.,

Although the Sibyls recognized *Apollo* and *Zeus* politically, they never accepted his predominance over *Mami*. Nonetheless, it was perhaps the threatening invasions from the barbarous northern Aryan tribes, which forced an uneasy political alliance between the Sibyls and the Egyptian Pharaohs. More significantly, the usurpation of their temples by a fanatical, patriarchal sect of the priest of Amon earned them the wrath and contempt of *Mami*.[58]

We are told that under the patriarchs, the nations had become completely corrupted. During prophetic pronouncements, the divine oracles of Mami, speaking through the Sibyls would always express Her disapproval of their actions in Her greetings to them.

Routinely, She would commence her oracles with the following greeting:

"Mortal men! Bodies of clay, vile nothings, how can ye dare to elevate yourselves, and why do ye not think of the end of the world? "[59]

Angered by the usurpation of Her temples and the general corruption wrought throughout the land, The Divine African Mother prophesied through her Sibyls, great woes on the matriarchal cities of *Lycia, Smyrna Ephesus,* Corinth and others where Her temples had been seized and corrupted.

Unlike what has been accepted as "*biblical*" prophecies today where the future of Africa and its peoples are mysteriously absent, the Sibyl prophecies, from which "*biblical*" doctrines are actually derived, were very specific to their own (African) people.

In the beginning, as their matriarchal kingdoms, divine power and political influence around the world began to grow, their prophecies became even more central to global events; and took on a more international, multiethnic tone. Particularly, as they faced the inevitable threat from the invading northern Aryan tribes. These tribes eventually were either absorbed by the matriarchs or they became the new conquerors. As these foreign tribes became the new rulers, the prophecies of the Sibyls became even more pronounced.

It is alleged that it was her anger at the seizure of her temples and the subsequent corruption that usually followed, why she allowed for Egypt and many of her African nations to fall victim to barbaric and foreign invasions; and ultimate ruin, as divine punishment. For example, in one (not so corrupted) prophetic verse, she proclaims through the Sibyl:

Alas for thee, O Libya! Alas for thee, O sea and Land in the Western Nations! How shall you come to the miserable day! You shall come exercised in a conflict which will be terrible and difficult, you shall have a fearful Judgement again, and you all shall come to destruction because you have destroyed the great Ammon Temple of the Immortal God;

grievously grinding it as it were with iron teeth; for this cause thou shalt see thy land filled with dead bodies, some slain in War, and all the force of evil spirits, by Famine and Plague, and by enemies of a barbarous fury. All thy land shall become a desert, and thy Cities be forsaken. [60]

Under patriarch, this as most of the Sibyl prophecies were altered to name the temple "*Amon,*" and substitute to "*Goddess*" to read as "*God.*" However, the omphaé temples in Libya were originally dedicated to *Athena, Minerva,* and *Poseidon.* Nonetheless, anywhere the sacred temples were violated, usurped, neglected or destroyed, these prophetic proclamations of doom were made.

In another pronouncement she further warns that:

In the West a star shall shine, which is called Comet, and is a sign of War, Famine, and death by Plague, and of the Slaughter of great commanders and nobleman, and there shall be other great signs among men: for the Meaotic Lake and deep Tanais shall not continue their flux of waters; and there shall be ploughed land in its channel; but the currents shall become innumerable. There shall be great openings of the Earth, and vast caverns shall appear, and men with their cities shall be swallowed up. These cities shall be overthrown in Asia [Minor], Jassis, Cerb, Pandonic, Colophos, Ephesus, Nicea, Antochcia, Tanagra, Sinope, Smynra, Marus; and these towns in Europe, Cyagra, Clitus, Basilis, Merope, Antigone, Magnesia, Mycene, Pantheia, wealthy Gaza, Hierapolis, and Astipalei. Then know thou that the pernicious People of Egypt are near destruction, and then the last year will be over with the Alexandrians. [61]

She foretold of famine, disease and pestilence and, it was usually during these end-cycles that She would speak of the coming of a "savior" from the East." Varro tells us this savior was *Ihsous,* or "*Khrisna*" claiming that he [the savior] would "dominate the whole, [and would become] a triumphant national hero."

Continuing with the fate of Egypt, she proclaims:

O Egypt! A terrible great slaughter shall befall thee, which thou didst hope will never befall thee. A sword shall pass through the midst of they lands, and dispersion, and death, and famine shall follow. But, in the seventh Generation of the Kings thou shalt have rest. [62]

She continues:

Woe to thee, O Land of Gog and Magog, lying between the Ethiopian Rivers! How great an effusion of Blood shalt thou receive! And men shall call thee the House of Judgement; and thy well-watered land shall drink black blood.

Mentioned in the Book of Ezekiel (38 and 39), "*Gog*," is a derisive corruption of the ancient African "*Gargars.*" Located in what is now the Armenian highlands, Gargars is a land-locked country bordering Turkey and Iran. The *Gargars* are also known as the "*Gargarensians*", and is also one of the ancient locations of the African, "Arap" (*Sabean/Ethiopian*) clans who founded the matriarchal, Mittani empire, and is known as the ancestral home of *Queen Nefertiti.   Gargars* was believed to be the actual location of *Mt. Arrata* (Arafat).

Just as their Elamite neighbors, *the Gargars'* ancestral home was probably *Sheba* (actually" *Saba*", meaning "*serpent-people*"). *Sheba* is the name of the ancient city that the lies "between the Ethiopian rivers" and ancient home of the Sibyl "*Makere, (Makeda)*, popularly known as "*Queen of Sheba.*"[62]

Opportunistic Rise of the Imperial Roman Papacy

Over the centuries the Sibylline prophecies began to take on a more global and nationalistic tone. As Africa began to lose her colonies and political and economic influence in Asia Minor and in the Mediterranean regions, the geo-political paradigm gradually shifted. During the Roman era, particularly as the Roman Church changed from an apostolic (secular) body to an expansionist, Imperial power, there is a conscious reassessment of Roman racial and cultural identity. Particularly its gradual shift from the worship and dependency on African god/dessess and sacerdotal authority to that of the newly emerging Roman papacy.

African matriarchal cultural and spiritual predominance, in existence since the beginning of time, began to be viewed by Roman authorities as a serious cultural liability, and an obstacle to the carefully veiled Eurocentric ecumenical ideals now being espoused by Greek philosophers and the Church papals. The Roman Church lacking an original ecclesiastical, liturgical and theological doctrine of its own, still depended heavily on the Sibylline prophecies and the African (including Buddhist), Judaic and Mithraic (Persians) religious customs in legitimizing its superior position over the competing Hebrew doctrines.

Fig 12: Sibyl image taken from a "Moor" (Phonencian) coat-of-arms. Draped around her neck is the serpent of the original *Adim/Adama*, known in ancient Egypt as "Osiris, and later as the ancestral *Aesculapius*, *Dionysus Attis*, etc. In ancient Egypt and Ethiopia, these Sibyl oracular priestesses were known as the *'Black Doves.'* They were also called *"Pythias"* or *"Python Priestesses."* Their accurate prophecies originally meant for the ancient, African world, were later plagiarized by the Levites (Hebrews), and later by the Roman Church, and attributed to non-African male prophets. By default, the Sibyl prophecies and oracles were directly instrumental in building the ecclesiastical foundation of Christianity, and for shaping the geopolitical dynamics of the ancient world.

The new, Euro-patriarchal *"World Order"* could no longer afford to tolerate the notion of relying on African, matriarchal divine predominance as its fundamental theological and cultural base. Unlike seizing the spoils of war, the African divinities whose mysteries the Romans did not understand were ancestrally linked and thus, its divine power could never be completely usurped and controlled by them.

Furthermore, the patriarchal Hebrew Shepards, whose holy laws and canons do *not* predate the prophecies of the Sibyls, also revolted against them, and they later came to be known historically as the *Semitic* Jews of Palestine. They had long ago broken away from the matriarchal orders and, following the historic trend began by the patriarchal priests of Horus, and the Babylonian Marduk, the

Jews did away with the worship of their primary black goddess, *Anath-Yahu*, (*Yahweh*) and elevated her minor consort "*Jehovah*" in her place.[63] They too were competing with the Roman Church for patriarchal dominance in the world.

However, the Jews inheritors of a theological foundation originally established by the African matriarchs, were entirely familiar with African theology, philosophy and sacred rites. However, in their revolt against them, they needed their own male god and "*Messiah*" to prove the legitimacy of their newly "*chosen status,*" as well as to free them from Roman oppression and tyranny. Both groups (Jews and Roman papacy), wasted no time in seizing, plagiarizing and ultimately destroying the original Sibylline prophecies. By replacing them with corrupted or complete forgeries to meet their own politico-religious agenda, they then flooded the global community with these bogus doctrines, adding further to the confusion in their on-going propaganda wars against the Roman papacy.

More significantly, by proclaiming the prophetic messages of the Sibyls entirely to themselves as the "chosen ones," helped to undermine and to conceal the African specificity and spiritual identity of the Sibyls. In doing so, the original message and target of the Sibyl prophecies has been obscured and lost over the centuries, thus omitting an extremely critical historical element of African ecclesiastical and prophetic history.

The Sibylline oracles were deliberately doctored to attack the very essence of African philosophy, theology, ritual and liturgical practices, of whom the Sibyls were the very epitome. More revealing, it redirected their prophetic messages away from the African kingdoms, villages and nation heads for whom it was originally intended. What remained instead was a wholesale condemnation of African spirit and culture, with an external focus exclusively on the messianic hopes of the very (Jwish and Roman papal) forces responsible for its destruction.

Additionally, all of the major prophecies of the Sibyls demanded these propitiation, sacrifices to appease the African gods, goddess and ancestors, which was yet another source of contention with the Christian papal who bitterly denounced and rejected them as "*heathen abominations.*" Consequently, the papacy rushed to either destroy or to remove these crucial utterances from the Sibyl prophecies as well.

Though the Jews and the Roman papal authorities were competing enemies, both were in agreement that the African, divine matriarchal authority had to be discredited and ultimately destroyed. The motivations of the Jews stemmed from their hatred of the Divine African Mother and their bitter break with the patriarchal, pharaonic orders of ancient Egypt. The Roman Church's usurpation of her sacerdotal power was motivated out of nothing less than mere political expediency and economic necessity.

In the end, what remained for the African was a corruption of their own spiritual doctrines, in which the prophecies of the Sibyls were rewritten to forecast Levitical Jews waiting for their "*Jehovah*" and the Christians waiting for their "*second coming of Christ.*"—while the African people and others, are left begging for the crumbs of "*salvation*" that would fall from the table, of what amounts to little more than a politically orchestrated doctrinal and historical lie. All told, there remains scant credible evidence from either of these groups of the existence of an ancient omnipotent power independent of the Divine African Mother.

Though the Sibyls had lost much of their global kingdoms and international influence, their spiritual advice, healings and prophecies were still being sought by military leaders, heads of state and nobility, albeit, under the cover of night.

Those Sibyls who were not as prominent, simply faded away into their rural villages, sacred caves, mystery schools, grottos and "g*hettos.*" Their prophecies now being universally discredited in the ancient world as the work of "*crazed women, harboring demonic spirits*".

However, this perception would change temporarily, as a new generation of Roman patricians came of age.

It is important to note that these African-centered prophecies were said to have been given over a period of more than 4,000 years. Centuries before the alleged era of the Hebrew prophets or any concept of Christianity, Hindu-ism or Islam, were ever conceived. The Sibyls claimed in one prophecy that their genesis began in the *"tenth age of the world, during which time, Saturn, Titan and Japhet were born from the union of heaven and Earth.* She recounts in detail about the divine lineages of Saturn and all the misfortunes that would befall them in the war of the Titans; and the ultimate division of the world amongst the children of *Jupiter, Neptune and Pluto.*[64.]

In the above allegory, the Sibyl appears to be making reference to a mythological story of Saturn, whom having stolen the rightful succession to the throne from his oldest brother Titan, due to the manipulations of Saturn's wife Rhea. Titan then declared war against Saturn, defeated him and held Saturn and his brother captive, until Jupiter (Titan's elder son) became a man and released them from their captivity. As a reward, the world was then divided amongst Titan's sons, *Jupiter, Neptune and Pluto.*

Placed back into African cosmology, the *Titans* and Titanesses, or *"divinities/ lords"*, are the ancient African pantheon of the seven celestial deities from the Pleiades star system, who were served by the Sibyls. They were introduced into Babylonian and Palestinian astrology by the *Afro-Canaanite/Phoenician* matriarchal clans who settled into ancient Corinth around 2000 B.C.E. Seven became the mystical number of the ancestral deity *Dionysus*, and later, was applied to the minor fire deity, *Jehovah*. It was also the number by which the African solar gods were torn into pieces and resurrected again, *Osiris* being the first.

The *"division of the world"* was believed to be making reference to the fall of the *'Tower of Babel'* in ancient Babylon, resulting in the rise of (a second) *Egypt, Persia and Medea, Ethiopia* and later Assyria, Macedonia and then Rome.[65] It appears to also be making direct reference to the fall of the African matriarchies resulting in the rise of the patriarchs, and the subjugation of African female spiritual and political power, creating a permanent division or fragmenting of the African Sibs.

However, around 573-808 B.C.E, with the raging wars and bitter feuding between the Levitical Hebrews and Romans, the "*heathen*" prophecies of the Sibyls had proved so accurate and of such global and religious significance that the patriarchal world again began to take notice.

Today, in western history and mythological literature, originally meant to conceal their African identity, the Sibyl's sacred temples are obscurely referred to as simply "*oracles.*" However, as the main centers of African spiritual life, they were clearly much more than that; and will henceforth be referred to in their current African religious vernacular as "*shrines*" "*egbes,*" or "*temples*".

Additionally, it is important to note that these Sibyl prophetess and the "*miracles,*" that they performed, were never viewed from an African world view, as something *extraordinary, remarkable* nor *as even miraculous.*

This attitude was not borne out of disrespect, but rather, when placed within their own religio-cultural African context, direct contact "with the spirits (divine phenomena) was common and rather routine in their daily lives. They were not magical manifestations typically meant to awe or to entertain. Just as today, it was even considered almost sacrilege either to speak directly about them or to take them out proportion.

It was the Europeans, specifically the Greeks and later the Romans, who found African ritual and spiritual phenomena "*extraordinary,*" and later through the auspices of the Roman church, began to categorized them as "*miracles,*" making much-ado about something viewed as common by the African.

For the African, the so-called "spiritual phenomena" was never viewed as important as the actual divine message, and the sacrifices that were needed to appease the anger of the ancestors and their tutelary deities.

HISTORICAL SIBYLS: PRIESTESSES OF MAMI

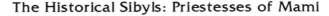

The Historical Sibyls: Priestesses of Mami

Fig 13: Sybil prophetess, mis-classified simply as
"*Female figure*." Her arms close to her heart and bodice
meaning that she is *keeper of the mysteries*.
Greek, Archaic ca. 650 B.C.E Louvre, Paris.

Know them by Name

Note: *Many of these dates cannot be confirmed and seem to contradict, either the era of nations, and rulers, or simply are too far in ancient history to be connected with any recordable event. So much of what remains of the lives of the Sibyls are from secondary and tertiary sources. The Catholic church and its revisionist writers have harbored a monopoly on these African High Priestesses since they seized total power and oversaw the destruction of their mystery schools, temples and libraries. However, this should by no means invalidate who they are and their absolute critical, and historical significance in linking African divine spirit, throughout the fabric of all of world history. What is also certain, is that the African Divine Spirit that guided them rests in the blood and ancestral soul of all African people. This ancient tradition still exists, in the Mami-Isis, Mami Watas, and others in West Africa and in the Diaspora.*

Overview

Just as there were many male prophets during ancient times but only a few were distinguished from amongst them, this same tradition held true of the Sibyls. Although they maintained grand temples to Mami, and the ancestral, oracular solar/sun serpent deity. And their divine words, prophecies and wisdom was quoted, honored and revered all throughout the ancient world, less than a dozen were elevated to renowned status during any given time period.

Plato, Justin and Arisophanes tell us that:

... the Sibyls were not a few; all of them embracing the same Prophetic life; and for some particular reason ... they all chose the appellation of Sibyls... A tradition by the inhabitants, which came down to them from their [African] ancestors. [66]

However, the identity of literally hundreds of these original divine African goddesses will never be known. Their prophecies and history stolen and plagiarized. Their African statues and faces destroyed or deliberately obscured. Many overlaid with fake Arab, Greek, and Roman images, reflecting centuries of foreign invasions, cultural theft and hostile occupations.

Although the Sibyls were known to the non-African ancient world only as "prophetesses", all throughout ancient Africa, they were revered as divine. The great mother healers, diviners and sages, who literally gave birth to the gods; and aligned their people to their own personal destiny, divinity and to their ancestors. The Sibyls were descendants of the first pre-historic matrilineal order of so-called "serpent worshiping" clans, of whom all African queens/queen mothers and the ecclesiastical order of priestesses and diviners, healers, artisans and stone builders were born.

It was these warrior queens who fled in droves from Libya, Ethiopia, Uganda, Nubia, southern Syria (Elam) and Babylon, into Asia Minor, Ionia and ancient Mycenea to join their African and Dravidian sisters who had already established a new home for the African Gods/dess after the Great Flood.[67] In the "New World" during transatlantic slavery, it was the descendants of these women and male priests and devotees, who jumped into the oceans, rather than serve under another wave of colonial invaders.

Just as in the modern-day Mami Wata Vodoun tradition, the Sibyls honored as "Togbui, Amengansie, Hounon, Mama, Queen Mother" etc., were high priestesses. The majority were even married and bore children; and most were required to be over the age of fifty. This tenant came about after the rape of a very young Sibyl priestess some centuries ago at the shrine in Delphi. Afterwards, it was decreed that they must all be past their childbearing years.

This historical fact, was unknown to later Church revisionists, when they began concealing and obscuring the Sibyl's African identity by referring to them as "white, chaste, youthful virgins". In ancient Greece, the Sibyls were also known as "Pythia, Pythoness and Pythians," because of the presence of the ancestral, father python serpent. The most ancient of their shrines were at Delos. It was claimed to be where the Black Di-ana (as Ar-temis) was born, and later, after the seize of her temples, Apollo and Zeus' names were added to the list as their "original" birth home.

The following Sibyls being described are also historically listed based upon the country in which they were born, or where they were said to have prophesied. Depending upon which location and the deity of which they served, the name "Sibyl " might be phonetically changed into "Cybele or Sellae, and Helli, Elli for the males. Some of the African male prophets have even been called "Tomuri, Tomurrare, Tomurus," to denote the sacred temple located at the foot of the mountain Thesprotia[68] located in north west Greece, near the river Acheron.

The sacred river Acheron (or "river of woe") was the historic location of one famous carven of the Sibyls who called-up the souls of the dead. It was later demonized by the Roman papals and reclassified as one of the so-called "five rivers of Hades." The name "Tomurus" associated with the African order of sun priests, would later be corrupted into the english *"Thomas"* (the Apostle) whose prophecies, just as the *Book of Enoch*, the *Book of Jubilees*, the *Book of Solomon*, the *Ascensio Moysis* and others have been denounced and excluded from the bible by the Roman papals as heresy.

The inherent benefit of this brief overview and chronology of the Sibyls, is that it offers the contemporary reader a global overview of the African, matriarchal presence and enormous influence they welded in the ancient world. Their great impact has always far exceeded the limited physical, cultural geographical and political designations of which Africa and the spiritual roles of which African women in particular, are confined today.

━━━━━━━━━━━

The Sibyls: A Brief Overview   (all dates are approximate)

Cumae (3364 B.C.E): *Herophile* (meaning *dear/initiated to the Mami goddess "Hera"*) Herophile is claimed to be from a province in Asia Minor (Turkey) known as Cumae. She was known by several names, *Amalthea, Phoemonoea, Heropila and Europa*, [from which *"Europe"* derives its name]. She was also known as *Demophile* and *Demo*. However, some historians suspect these to be the names of other Sibyls. *Cumae* is also claimed to be the Palestinian *Sabbe* (Cushite/black Sibyl).[69] She is one of the oldest and first of the two *"black doves,"* claiming to be the daughter or daughter-in-law of **Oannes,** whom they actually called *"IE/Ioa/, and present day Christians call "Noah."*

Cumae was a high priestess of the Mami deity *"Hera"*, (meaning *"Lady/ Protectress"*) who under African patriarchy, was later paired with as the *sister/wife* of the thunder god *Zeus. Cumae* lived in a cave during the time of Roman, *Tarquin the Elder.*

She is said to have also lived on the island of *Samos,* and to have traveled extensively throughout Asia Minor (Turkey). At Delphi during patriarchal occupation of the temples, *Cumae* is said to have sung endlessly to her sacred deity installed in the sacred omphaé.. In one of her favorite epitaphs, she sang:

I Sibylla, Phoibo's wise woman
am hidden under a stone monument:
I was a speaking virgin but voiceless
In this manacle by the strength of fate.
I lie close to the nymphs [Mami] and to Hermes
I have not lost my sovereignty.

The above song is a chant of political and spiritual protest, making direct reference to the takeover of the Sibyl temples by the priests of *Amon/Amen* (Apollo). In the above song, she is declaring where her true power and divine authority rests; meaning with Mami and Hermes, the healer and *opener of roads.* She also makes reference to the African ancestress title of *"Phoibo or* Phoebe," (meaning *"moon."* It is one of the sacred names of the *Black-Di-ana,* and an honorary title held by all *Sibyls.* However, Apollo's priests, having made the divine son equal to that of the mother, declared this same title for themselves, by altering it to the masculine *"Phoebus."*[70]

As high priestess of the underworld, one of *Cumae's* form of divination was with the sacred laurel leaf. She would write her prophecies on laurel leaves and leave them for the wind to scatter and fall into their own random order, at the entrance of her cave. In one account, *Cumae* reportedly gathered nine of her books and marched into town, and presented them to the first Afro-Etruscan king of Rome, *Tarquin,* for a price of three-hundred gold pieces. He, now *"christianized,"* casted dispersion upon her as a poor, black *"heathen,"* and refused to purchased them.

Angered, *Cumae* promptly set ablaze three of the sacred books of propehcies, and represented the remainder demanding the same price. Again, *Tarquin* refused.

Again *Cumae* proceeded to burn three more of her prophetic books, and again demanded the same price for the last remaining three.

Shocked and disturbed by *Cumae*'s persistence and mere audacity, Tarquin immediately consulted the Augurs (black diviners). The diviners admonished him for his disrespect of the great prophetess, and demanded that he quickly purchase the remaining three books. This Tarquin promptly did, and after examining them, he soon realized their great significance. According to the Roman historian, *Pliny*, those remaining three prophetic books were held in such high esteem, that they were placed in the Capitol, protected by fifteen guards appointed by Tarquin.[71]

Cumae's prophetic texts were only consulted in national crisis, and special permission (though never granted) had to be obtained to view them. Tarquin sent emissaries all over the black world visiting the "*heathen*" shrines of the Sibyls now scattered throughout the Roman appointed "African ghettos," to gather any remaining books. By then, the Jews (Hebrews) were already plagiarizing or making their own propaganda, passing them off as the authentic, Sibylline oracles.

What is being implied here, is that these prophetic books of the Sibyls became the sole and undisputed precursor to the western, Christian Bible. The prophecies, oracles and revelations of the Sibyls were systematically retrieved, purchased, stolen and haphazardly collected by various means all throughout the ancient world where their temples existed.

Many books were later plagiarized, revised or altered, and complied into one holy book known as the *Sibylline Oracles*. Those books that were used to compile what is known today as the Judeo-

Christian bible, were then credited exclusively to male prophets, or its author listed simply as "*unknown*." To further conceal the identity of its true authors, the gender of "*god*" was changed from feminine to masculine. Originally, within each prophetic verse, it is claimed the Sibyls made praises to "*Mami*" as "*Our Lady*," and proclaimed that she was "*greater than any other [god] in the world*."[72]

Those books for which it was hard to conceal their African matriarchal origins were simply destroyed, or relegated to heresy. Roman senator, Cicero,(*the orator)* writes that the last three books of *Cumae's* were deliberately burned in a fire by the Roman Governor, "*Stilicon the Tyrant*." *Stilicon* was eternally hated by all of Rome for this sacrilegious act, which prompted a universal reaction from poets, scholars and musicians alike. So worshiped was this Sibyl of Cumea, that she was immortalized in one of her appellations "*Europa*" for which Europe is allegedly named. Lydian, traveler and geographer, *Pausanias,* is said to have written that upon *Cumae's* death, her ashes were kept in an urn at the temple of Apollo.[73]

Erythrean/Ethiopian Sibyl: This Sibyl's name is recorded by Greek historians as "*Eriphyle*", or "*Erythrean*." According to the Greeks, "*Erythrean*" refers to the ancient name for the "*Indian Ocean*." Its location being where one of the temples from which this Sibyl either worked or was born.[74] This Ethiopian Sibyl was also one of the most famous known prophetess from the Delphi Shrine located in (the now biblical) Euphesus. *Eriphyle* is further reputed to be one of the oldest Sibyls from Africa. So old in fact, that she is claimed to be the actual daughter-in-law of Noah (*Ioah*) and a crowned priestess of *the Mami deity Ar-Themis* (Artemis/Black Di-Ana)[75] *Eriphyle* is also recorded as the second of the two " *black doves*", who was sent to find dry land and to found the holy oracle shrines at Delphi and at Dodona. According to Greek historian, and philosopher, *Strabo*, *Eriphyle* was "*one of the inspired and prophetic [African] women among the Ancients*."[76]

We are told that when *Eriphyle* first came out as an initiated prophetess, "*she foretold everyone's destiny,[referring to them] by name. She foretold what should befall them and delivered it in verse (parable) and that after some time she recovered her human form again.*"[77]

According to Afro-Greek historian *Apollodorus* (2 cen. B.C.E.), who was then a native of Ionia, *Eriphyle* foretold of the Greek's invasion of (then) *Ethiopian* Tory, and predicted their miliary success. She also foretold that the Greek poet, *Homer,* would someday write a number of books of fiction. She admonished him in advance of what he would do once the Greeks became firmly established in ancient Troy. She predicted that he would build his literary career by studying and then plagiarizing her prophetic words, and by copying her poetic style claiming it as his own. *Eriphyle*'s prediction came true when Homer published his famous poem *the Odyssey*. Hailed as the first "*great work of Western literature*", these two poems based on Afro-Grecian gods and religious culture, set the standard for Western epic poetry. So depended upon were the prophetic versus of this African Sibyl, that the Roman Senate reportedly sent fifteen ambassadors to the city where *Eriphyle* resided to obtain her verses to place in the Roman Capitol.[78] The above information is all that remains on the life of *Eriphyle*. There is no current record of how *Eriphyle* 's life ended.

Hellespontica (500 B.C.E?): *Hellespontica* is said to have been born in a Trojan war camp called *"Marmesso"*, during the reign of Cyrus, then king of Persia (Iran). The Persians who envied and despised the Egyptians and Ethiopians, finally captured many of their major Grecian and other Mediterranean colonies, enslaving its black inhabitants and forcing many into "camps." The Persians were alleged to have taken *Hellespontica*'s extraordinary praises for the *Black Di-ana* (or Isis) and put them in the mouth of the "*Virgin Mary*," known to the Afro-Asian ancient world to be a factitious Western concept. The above information is all that remains on the life of *Hellespontica*. Her ancient depiction was one of an elderly black woman carrying sheaves of corn as the Ethiopian, Mami deity *Kore*.

There is no current record of how *Hellespontica*'s life ended.

Samia (294 B.C.E ?):   *Samia* is said to be from the Grecian Islands of *Samos*, one of the earliest settlements of the black, Libyan matriarchal clans who emigrated there around 2500 B.C.E *Samia* was also known as *Heriphila*. She was said to have lived during the time of the black, Roman *King Numa Pompilius*. She is quoted by early Roman writers such as *Sozomeno, Suydas, Nicephorus*. There is no current record of how *Samia's* life ended.

Fig 14: Pre-Grecian islands and parts of Asia Minor showing African matriarchies during Greek and later Persian occupation. The ancient Ethiopian clan of *Phyrgians* (now Western Turkey) are mentioned by the Sibyls to be the oldest inhabitants on earth.

Phrigia/Phyrgia (2996 B.C.E): Phyrgia was a high priestess of the *Black-Di-ana/Ar-Themis (Artemis/Cybele)*. She as her name implies, was claimed to be a *Phrygian*, one of the indigenous black, proto-Elamite clans of Asia Minor. Her mother was said to be *Dardanus* and her father was a black, Turkish king named, *Neso*. Phyrgia lived in the small city of *Anzira*, and was said to be prophesying at (or sometime before) the era of King Solomon. Phyrgia is credited with the same miracles and prophecies of her predecessors. Depending on who's writing the history, she is also claimed to be the first. There is no current record of how life Phyrgia ended.

Libyan Sibyl (2815 B.C.E?): Her name is given by Franciscan monks, (her chief rivals), as *Bybissa* or *Elisa*. There is no known record of how *Bybissa* worked nor how she lived. However, what is recorded is that centuries later, Bybissa's prophetic verses would be been badly plagiarized and corrupted by pope Sixtus V, (1521-90 C.E.).

Namely, the usual altering of the Sibyl's prophetic words and spiritual works; and crediting them to their own Christian "*prophets*," and to their "*Christ*." In one alteration, Sixtus places into the mouth of Bybissa' that a [Christian] "*savior*," would come and "*heal the sick, make the blind see, the lame walk*," etc.,. The obvious flaw with this, is that these "miracles" the Sibyl themselves did, and had been doing for centuries. Sixtus further has *Bybissa* prophesying that this "*savior*" would "*recline His sacred limbs on the lap and arms of the Queen of Heaven.*" This attribute is only given to the queen mother, priestesses and prophetesses of *Mami-Isis*, known by her many names, most notably in ancient Greece as the "*Black Di-Ana.*"[74] There is no current record of how Bybissa's life ended.

Themis of Delphi: (2802 B.C.E): *Themis* is said by Roman and Greek historians to have been born at *Delphos* (Boeotia, Greece) and that her name was *Themis* or *Anthemis*, an initiated priestess of *Ar-themis*. *Themis* was said to be the daughter of the famous black, Theban diviner and priest, *Tyresias*, and his high priestess wife, *Daphne*. She is reputed to have prophesied before the destruction of Ethiopian, Troy, and to have written about Priam, the black, king of Troy, and his main wife *Hecuba*. Namely, during the Trojan wars, Priam's alliance of *Paris* and *Helen*, two ancient black, provinces in Troy. It is this Sibyl that Homer is alleged to have also plagiarized her prophecies to write the *Iliad*. Themis was worshiped all throughout ancient Rome, where a statue was built in her honor.[75] It was in a province called *Georgis* in Troy, that *Themis* was known as "*Georgthian*, and a sepulcher to her was built in the temple of Apollo. It was also in this city where coins were minted of her, alongside an engraving of the Sphinx. There is no current record of how Themis' life ended.

Sambetha of Persian/Persica (2769 B.C.E): Also known as *Chaldea* and *Helrea,* her name is given by Franciscan monks as *Sambetha*. She is claimed by the Roman Catholic papals to be the "*first prophetess.*" *Sambetha* is said to be the daughter of the black, Chaldean historian, *Beroso,* and her mother Erimanta.

The Shrine location from which *Sambetha* came was a Mami shrine to *Astarte*. However, mention is made of *Sambetha* by Nicanor, Greek historian of *Alexander the Great*, in which her prophesies had been altered to have predicted the coming of a Christian "*savior,*" "*John the Baptiste,*" and of the "*death and crucifixion*" of this savior.

It is important to keep in mind that punishment by crucifixion was originally a black, *Phoenician (Carthaginian), Canaanite* practice, adopted centuries later by the Romans. These Sibyls too were also African, and the subject of their prophecies were as a rule, devoted to their own people and to their own priestly orders. Therefore, the above allegations by Nicanor, and much of what *Sambetha* had originally prophesied and to whom she was actually referring, had long been corrupted by the Roman papals. This Sibyl prophetess, *Sambetha* is claimed to have written eighty-four books of prophecy, now all allegedly "destroyed". She is said to have lived a long time. There is no record of how or where is died.

Sibyl of Cumea/ Cimera (600-700 B.C.E): No exact birth date has been given, but this Sibyl prophetess is claimed to have been around during the time of the black Roman legislature, and King Numa Pompilius, who was also a priest of the water goddess *Egeria*. However, she is believed to be a different Sibyl from the Sibyl at Cumae in Asia Minor (Turkey). This Sibyl of Cumae is of *Cimera*, a small province in Campana, Italy. She was called *Cimeria*, or *Chimita*, but was said to have been born in Babylon. *Cimeria* is said to also be the daughter of a *Berosus*, the black historian who wrote the history of the Chaldeans. However, this might be mere speculation, because some accounts have Berosus to have lived between(330-260 B.C.E).

Cimeria is said to have lived in a cliff cavern on Mount Gaurus, several miles from Cumea in Rome. Many Sibyls came and went from this region, but not all were endowed with the gift of divination or prophecy. One Siby named, *Deiphobë,* even allegedly lived to one-hundred ten years and remained enshrined in the cave.

As did most heads of state, Roman, Emperor Claudius recounts having visited *Cimeria* after his ascendency to the throne. According to him, "*before being permitted to visit the Sibyl, I had to sacrifice a bullock [castrated bull] and an ewe [sheep] . . . to Apollo and to Artemis respectively.*"[79]

Cimeria is said to be the prophetess to have "*conducted Aeneas' [ritual] descent into hell.*" The more likely scenario is that *Cimeria* served as the ceremonial priestess who conducted the rites of the dead, so that Aeneas, who as a priest of Mami, would have a successful voyage back to the world of the ancestors. In the Catholic "*Mass of the Dead*" they have a line which reads "*Test David cum Sibylla,*" which they attribute to *Cimeria.*[80]

Pagan turned "Christian," St. Justin (100 C.E.), tells us that *Cimeria* "*used to ascend [to] some high place and teach the people.*" More importantly, it was this Sibyl who first divided her prophecies by designating the nation epochs by metals. Roman poet, Virgil, (70 BC-19 B.C.E.), who is alleged to have actually seen the original books, (and even plagiarized some of her prophecies), claimed in his *Aeneid*, that *Cimeria* divided them into the age of "*Iron . . . Gold . Bronze* etc." A prophetic book which is now allegedly "destroyed," and the credit for designating nations to metals is now given to the Christian "prophet" Daniel, for the" *Book of Daniel*", and to "St. John", for the *Book of Revelation.* The Romans credit *Cimeria* with prophesying the birth of *Julius Caesar* and his nephew *Augustus.* The famous black augur/diviner Navius, speaks about *Cimeria* in his book on the Punic Wars.[81] There is no record of how or where *Cimeria* died.

Sibyl of Tiburtina (30 B.C.E): She is claimed to be a native of Tiber (Tibur/Tivoli), a city outside of Rome. She was known by the name *Albumea/Albinaea.* She prophesied during the reign of Augustus Caesar. The "*vision*" of the "*black Madonna and Child*" is one he experienced while in a "*heathen temple,*" before the invention of the "*Virgin Mary.*" The Black Madonna is depicted carrying a palm branch, which later became one of the emblematic symbols of the Western Christ. *Albumea* was later worshiped as a divinity, where a shrine was built for her in a community near the Annis river.

This shrine was, as were others, eventually seized by the order of *Catholic Observants of St. Francis* and incorporated as most of its religious attributions credited to the white "Virgin Mary." *There is no record of how or where Albumea* died.

The Sibyl Agripina: She is said to have been a native, black Egyptian, and was called *Egypcia, Agrippa* or *Sanbera* and Norsica. Nothing is known of this Sibyl, except that she was quite recent in history. *Agrippa* was merely referred to as *"The Sibyl of Norsica."* Norsica a city in Perugia, Italy and is now a diocese. During the inquisitions (1500-1600s), and persecutions of African traditionalists, *Agrippa* lived in a cave and still tried to maintain a tradition of worship and initiations to Mami. She was constantly mocked and ridiculed by the locals as "insane," and as one who *"copulated with serpents."* By then, the papacy had succeeded in facilitating the downfall of the Sibyls, through widespread defamation. There is no record of how or where *Agrippa* died.

Priscilla (Prisca) and Maximilla: (240-250 C.E.)

These last two Sibyls are actually the ancient, African foremothers and father to the modern-day, black Charismatic *"Baptists and Pentecostals."* Because it is they, along with a priest named *Montanus,* all natives of Phrygia (now, western, Turkey), who first learned to adapt African spirits to the forced, Western "Christian" paradigm in the mid-second century C.E. Because the Roman imperial Church decided that after the *"Ascension of Christ,"* the *"Age of the Apostles; and the Age of Prophecy was over"*, they violently suppressed all African prophetic voices, especially those of the Sibyl priestesses. This group, as did other Africans, were still being born and called by their divinities, and thus founded *"The New Prophecy Movement,"* in which to voice their divine utterances. Although dubbed as *"Christian heresy"* by the Roman Imperial Church, *Montanus* and the Sibyl priestesses undeterred, forged ahead.

The patriarchal, papal authorities, refusing to accept a black woman's gift of prophecy, instead credited her divine utterances to *Montanus* proclaiming that:

Behold, man is as a lyre and I play upon him as with a plectrum; man sleeps and I arouse him; behold, it is the Lord who throws men's souls into ecstasy and gives them a heart."[82] [bold italics mines]

Fig 15: 199-217 C.E. Roman Catacomb of Sibyl priestess *Priscilla* (Prisca) and Maximilla. When the black matriarchs lost their sacerdotal and political powers in Rome, many were murdered, probably for "heresy."

Gender code words such as "*Man*" and "*Lord*," that did not exist until the advent of patriarchy, are clearly edited versions of the Sibyl's original prophecies, which always made reference to the divine Mother. Masculine pronouns were inserted by Church officials to render them consistent with their own corrupted Church doctrines.

In spite of this, the black, *Montanus* movement quickly spread in the African and Diaspora religious communities all throughout Europe, Asia and North Africa. So afraid and alarmed at being exposed, Roman Church officials haphazardly and routinely rounded these followers up, and tried to "*exorcize*" the divine African spirits, now classified as "*demons*," from them. When that didn't work, they simply had these followers *excommunicated* accusing them of *heresy.*

expressing the general sentiment of the Roman papals, and patricians against these African women, Roman "theologian", Hippolytus (d. c.236), categorically denounced the Sibyls, claiming that:

> . . . they [Montanist] have learned more from these [women] than from the law and prophets and the gospels. But they magnify these wretched women above the Apostles and every gift of Grace, so that some of them presume to assert that there is in them something superior to Christ.

What angered imperial Church officials the most, was the audacity of the Sibyls to structure their Church hierarchy in the original African matriarchal Sibs, and to elevate "*Eve*" (a disguise for *Mami*), above "*Adam*." This spurred Greek "theologian", *Eusebius* (c.263-339?), whom, fueled with misogynists rage to declare:

> . . the Montanists' [maintain] a special reverence for Eve because she ate from the tree of knowledge in the Garden of Eden. They acknowledge the sister of Moses as a prophetess in support of their practice of appointing women to the clergy . . . Women among them are bishops, presbyters, and the rest, as if there were no difference in nature.

Nonetheless, Hippolytus did convey that

> . . . they [prophetess] preached the end of the world, were the first to introduce dietary restrictions such as fasts and festivals, meals of parched food, and repasts [fast] of radishes, alleging that they [the Montanus] have been instructed by women [to do so]." (Ibidi).

Montanus preached for men and women to "*leave their spouses*" and to prepare for the "*new Jerusalem*", the "*Second Coming of Christ*," and to anticipate for the "*end of the world.*" This "*new Jerusalem*" Montanus was referring to, was not the *Jerusalem* during the time of "*Dud*" [King David], preached by Roman and Jewish clerics, but rather the "original *Jerusalem*," first built by the ancient *Oudes* (black Ethiopian Jews) who originated out of ancient India, and Afro-Syria. This particular sect worshiped the old black *Buddhists* religion which celebrated the divine African mother. The "*second coming*" preached by Montanus was referring to the 10th (or 11th) incarnation of the solar/son savior prophesied by the ancient Sibyls.

However, these critical theological distinctions became blurred and completely lost, as Roman and Jewish hegemony began to dominate the ancient world, and their relentless campaign of destroying the books, prophecies, traditions and temples of the old African goddesses, and replacing it with their exclusive religious propaganda.

After Montanus' death the Sibyls restructured the church and added their own scriptures, and excluded the Western Christian version which they believed to be fraudulent. They maintained a rigorous legalistic moral code, discouraged second marriages, and encouraged martyrdom when threatened. Their charismatic church of "*trance possession and prophecy,*" was so popular, that the Afro-Roman theologian, *Tertullian*, left the imperial Roman Church and went back to his ancestral homeland of Carthage and joined them. A nation where the religion quickly flourished.[83]

This deliberate act of cultural and religious militancy by *Tertullian*, embarrassed the Roman church, and made it even harder for the imperial papal authorities to destroy the Montanist Movement. Instead, the church papals simply chose to ignore them. Over the centuries, as patriarchal control and the suppression of women in Africa became standard cultural fare, the Montanist churches began to reflect this. More men and less female clergy were appointed, and it soon became simply another patriarchal, religious sect, in support of the Catholic church and the current status quo.

The Final Destruction of the Sibyl Prophecies and the Dilemma of Rome and the Papal Church

The *Sibylline Books* were rendered in the same, exact poetic and symbolically rich language which was considered the trademark of the first Sibyl priestess, *Phoemonoea*. This style was used as a measure of authenticity of any prophetic document written during the pre-Christian era. However, after all was said and done, the warring patriarchal factions of the *Levitical* Hebrews and those of the budding Christian papals, began creating a flood of confusing and contradictory forgeries, espousing their own brand of dogma and attributing them to the Sibyls.

Fig 16: Fragments of *"The Sibylline Oracles"* reprinted here by Milton Terry, are all that remains of the prophecies of the African Sibyl prophetesses, whose sacerdotal power and matriarchal kingdoms once ruled the ancient Mediterranean world for more than 6,000 years. Nearly all of their prophecies have been either destroyed, rewritten, altered or woefully corrupted at the hands of both their Jewish and Christian rivals, to reflect their own patriarchal bias and religious agendas. Even until today, the Sibyl's African identity has been completely omitted in which they are claimed in modern literature to be either non-African *"Greek,", Roman," "Jewish," "Persian"* or even simply being described as *"white virgin Christians*(!)."

This was the motivating impetus behind "St. John", alledge author of the *Book of Revelation*, a prophetic text which many in the ancient world believe was actually authored by the Sibyl *Herophile/ Phoemonoea*, when he makes the astounding threat that

" . . . I solemnly swear, if anyone adds anything to what is written, God shall add to him the plagues written in this book." Rev 22:16-19.

A typical preemptive threat employed by the warring Christian, and Jewish sects, both of whom were widely disseminating corrupted and altered Sibyl texts.   One of the main issues of contention in establishing Levitical and Christian legitimacy, was in changing the name *"Ixhousa"* whom the Sibyls stated would be the next *"savior"*and replacing it with that of either *"Jesus"* or *"Yahweh/Jehovah."*   *"Ixhousa"* appears to be an Afro-Chaldean name, similar to *"Xisuthros,"* the Mami *"fish"* deity later known as *Oannes.*

Higgins asserts that :

The pagan [Sibyl] prophecies being much clearer than those of the Jews. The [Platonists] philosophers annoyed because they clearly foretell a great person to come, and unless they allowed it to be Jesus Christ, they could make nothing of them. [84]

Another crucial factor which created a political and theological dilemma for both of these groups, was that these prophecies, spanning more than 4, 000 years, were inherently intended for the African nations and their clerics, where the major temples of the black goddess, and the temples of Amon, stretching from *Egypt, Israel, Turkey, Greece* and *Rome,* were addressed cyclically, by her.

The Sibyls were African and were the main oracle of the *"Serpent worshiping tribes,"* thus their prophetic "Spirit" was indeed an ancestral serpent, who had issued forth these divine prophecies, since the beginning of time. The Church papals knew this but had already condemned the serpent spirit as a manifestation of the highest evil.

Rome Reneges on Promise to Divine African Mother

Meanwhile, as the Roman patricians remained busy expanding its empire and consolidating its power, the social, economic and political climate began to change in Rome.   The Roman Church had long ago removed itself from being simply an apostolic local center of power. It became more concerned with territory, and acquiring wealth, and with gaining absolute control as an imperial world power.

By the sixth century C.E., patriarchal Africa, who had acquired much of its political and economic power by usurping the African matriarchs, and later through miliary expansion, had lost much of its economic and political predominance in the ancient world. Many of the African temple priests and priestesses, accustomed to expensive gifts, entertaining high dignitaries and other such luxuries, succumbed to complete corruption.

The African clergy began opening the temples only on certain days, and charging exorbitant prices for ceremonies and sacrifices; making them accessible only to the elite. An entire crop of foreign imposters having purchased initiations to acquire economic clout and social status, passed themselves off as authentic *"Sibyls, Bakides, Cueres,* (priests) and *diviners,* creating fringe cults and bizarre systems of rituals and worship; where many of the sacred laws and taboos were being ignored or violated.

Additionally, a new generation of *Caesars, Christians* and politicians, nurtured on a racist diet of political and religious propaganda, born from Greek and Roman philosophers and theologians, were espousing a more supremacist doctrine which entailed divorcing themselves from all *foreign,* especially African religious and cultural influences.

Constantine I, the first *"Christian"* and *pagan* emperor, reigned as a priest of *Sophia* (Artemis/Black Di-ana). Claiming black, Hellenic matriarchal lineage, Constantine maintained the festivals to her but, fearing a resurgence of the old matriarchal divine orders, he outlawed, on penalty of death, all forms of divination, ancestral sacrifices and festive ceremonies.

He knew these sacerdotal functions could only be performed through lineage, African priests/esses which included the *Sibyls/Pythoness/|Pythias*, which would quickly usurp the authority of the Roman papals, and they were therefore outlawed.

Fig 17: 400 C.E. Roman Catacombs of black Roman citizen, carrying religious offering. The level of persecution was such that many of the devotees of the Sibyls and others suffered horribly under the Imperial Church in Rome. Most resorted to clandestine meetings in the underground Catacombs to honor their African ancestors, deities and martyrs.

Broken Promises:
Sibyl Goddess Curses Rome

Constantine who once tolerated for political reasons African and other religious traditions, also began a campaign of destroying all of the African temples and shrines, especially in Asia Minor (Turkey). He finished off the final desecration at Delphi, by pillaging and carting off all of its art, books, and statuaries to adorn his new "Christian" temple at Constantinople (Turkey). Later he and his Christian emissaries invaded, destroyed and pillaged Carthage, and the temple of Tanit. These deliberate acts of sacrilege negated a centuries old promise made by the earlier Caesars to the black goddess, *Di-Ana*, that Rome would never invade or destroy Carthage, nor to persecute her people.

However, under the current, emperor *Julian* (361-63 C.E.), Constantine's nephew, he tried to maintain this promise, and attempted to restore many of Black Di-Ana's temples, but he only lived two years. The political process arguing the continued destruction, or attempts to revive African religious customs and institutions throughout Rome and her colonial territories, shuffled back and forth in the Roman Senate for decades.

Determined to rid Rome and "Europe" of African matriarchal and spiritual dependency, Roman general, Theodosius I (d. 376 C.E.), promptly confronted the Senate, who for twelve hundred years, kept their promise to the African Mother. He demanded the they stop financial support of the African temples to hold festivals to the African Goddesses, and to others gods. The senate responded that the African gods had blessed them immensely and that they would continue to bring money to the African priests for the usual sacrifices.[85]

The infamous Theodosius responded that they should embrace Christianity, claiming that the Roman treasury had no further funds for making the annual sacrifices. Thus, the edict "*religio-paganorum*," had been issued, classifying African based traditions as "*heathenistic and pagan.*" In the year 451 C.E. by pain of death, all forms of foreign and African religion, were outlawed by a constitutional amendment, under emperor and cousin of *Theodosius*, *Valentinian III.* General *Stilicho* (*a Gual/German*), by imperial decree struck a major blow when he demolished the temple of Apollo.

The final death blow was delivered by *Theodosius*, and his sons, during the reign of emperor *Valentinian I.* (321-75 C.E.) Now, backed by the full support of the Roman senate, *Theodosius*, in a violent wave of delight and fury, began in Egypt, where he closed and destroyed all of *Isis/Black Di-Ana's* temples, before turning his virulent rage against those remaining temples in Rome.

Temple reports:

Among the unspeakable crimes being referred to was the destruction by Bishop Theodosius of the Great Library of Alexandria because it contained 'heathen literature,' which . . . so often took place at the hands of fanatical a Christian Bishop attempting to wipe out all traces of history before Christ, and not as a result of an accidental fire . . . as the story is usually told.[88]

All throughout Africa especially, the Romans destroyed all of Mami's major temples and established *"monks and hermits"* or they urinated and defecated in its ruins, to make certain the Africans did not rebuild them.[86]   In their diabolical mayhem, they also destroyed the remaining *Sibylline oracles* anywhere that they found them, especially in Rome.   More than 300 years after the death of Christ, Rome was now officially a *"Christian"* nation, and all forms of divination, rituals and sacrifices were strictly prohibited.

From that moment onwards, according to some accounts, Rome began to experience all forms of misfortunes.[87] Because of these crimes and the   promises not kept by Rome to the Divine African Mother, the African Spirits were inconsolably grieved and angry.   Africans and those who followed the old religious order, were routinely denounced, ridiculed, persecuted, crucified and rendered ignorant *"heathens."* Subsequently, the Sibyls *"took great pleasures in forecasting the certain ruin of Rome."*

The Peculiar Dilemma of the Imperial Papacy

With the old African traditions well suppressed, the Roman Papal still had one major problem. They could not get around the undeniable fact that the Sibyl prophecies were still the only legitimate authority of a high and divine order, being exploited by both (Roman and Jew/Hebrew) sides to advance their own political agendas. According to Higgins:

These [Sibyl] prophecies have been equally troublesome to the [Roman] priests and [Roman & Greek] philosophers. The divines would have been very glad of them, but the adoption of them carried with it the shocking consequence that God must have had such bad taste as to have preferred even the wicked [Sibyl] pagans to his own people.[89] (brackets mines).

The papal authorities' problems were further complicated by the fact, that most of the ritual remedies inherent and specific within the Sibyl prophecies, required the traditional sacrificial propitiation, of which only the Sibyls and other African priests could legitimately
perform.

The arrogant Roman papacy found the idea of "*animal sacrifice*" repulsive, and had to either categorically reject the oracles entirely discredit the Sibyls, or find a means to remove that specific requirement from the Sibyl's prophetic books completely. This ignorant and contemptuous attitude by them is reflected in the statement made by Bell:

How much soever they [the Sibyls] might pretend to prophesy, they could not have it by divine inspiration; for most of the oracles . . . when consulted by the Romans, directed to the most idolatrous and abominable rites . . . therefore if they [the Sybils] had the gift of prophecy they must have received it from diabolical or evil spirits.[90]

The attempt to remove all references to animal sacrifice created a flood of forged documents from both the Jewish and Roman camps. Both groups putting into the mouths of the Sibyls, contradictory and absurd, "*prophetic*" admonishments and arguments against "*idolatry.*" This caustic and convoluted propaganda worked in both of their interest. However, the Roman and Jewish clerics rationale in justifying the continued use of the black Sibyl prophecies was becoming more absurd and irrational by the minute. Consider the following:

Because Idolatry had been introduced in the world, and the Devil, to confirm the false divinities, found a great success in giving answers through the idols, in order that those who came to consult them should believe that these divinities were the true God. These answers were given in many temples of the idols, and the most remarkable ones were in Dodona, a province in Egypt, where, according to Diodorus Siculus, in the depth of a wooded forest there was a temple dedicated to Jupiter." [another name for Amon][91].

Theft, Plagiarisms, and other Exploitations of the Sibyl's Prophecies

We are told that St. Augustine, the "*great Doctor of the Christian Church,*" employed corrupted and plagiarized prophecies of the Sibyls in his twenty-two book treatise on *The City of God*. Similarly, the Sibyl's "*Fourth Eclogue,*" considered to be a masterpiece of "*pagan prophecy*", was massacred by the Roman poet, Virgil in his so-called "*Oratio ad sanctum coetum.*"

They were not alone, the list of writers who heavily quoted from these black prophetess included other church fathers who had formed a committee specifically to adulterate their sacred works. Included were *Clemens Alexandrinus*, Justin, Martyr, Athenagoras, *Theophilus of Antioch, Tertullian, Lactantius, Eusebius, St. Jerom, St. Austin and Tacitus, and others.* All of whom were hailed by the church fathers as a "distinguished body of *Sibyllists*." An appointment to the board of *Quindecimviri*, was considered a very high honor. Their main objective were in destroying their most threatening rivals, Judaism and African *"Idolatry,"* and employing both Judaism and the Sibyl prophecies in laying the eschatological, theological and philosophical foundation of Christianity.[92]

The Final Destruction

As stated earlier, as long as African deities remained the divine and prophetic authority in Rome, the ecclesiastical and political power would remain in the hands of the African priests/esses. This along with the Roman Patricians being unable to navigate around the many prophecies intended for the *"African pagan"* masses, frustrated Augustus.

To begin the dismantling of the African gods' hold on Rome, he issued a decree to destroy the Sibylline Oracles. He, then, proceeded to burn more than two thousand of them and forbade by punishment of death, the reading of the Sibylline books; he kept only those that could be altered or that addressed the ultimate fate of Rome.[93] These actions followed years of persecution, discrimination and social ostracism. Reminiscent of modern day politicians, each successive emperor promising to restore the old (Africans) gods in order to garner political support only to later renege on their promises.

The Christians, centuries later revised this history and proclaimed themselves as being the ones persecuted. However, the evidence reveals otherwise. One case in point, is when Roman emperor Nero (37-C.E. 68), after attempting to find some guidance in the Sibylline books that would calm the growing resentment and disconnect of the persecuted African and "gentile" masses, was hailed as a "hero" in the following praise song:

> Hail, Olympian Victor! Hail, Pythian Victor! Augustus! Augustus! Hail
> Nero, our Hercules! Hail Nero, our Apollo! The only Victor of the
> Grand Tour, the only one from the beginning of time! Augustus!
> Augustus! O, Divine voice! Blessed are they that hear thee![94]

It is obvious that these proclamations of gratitude and praise are not to "*Jesus,*" but rather to the lineage of the African ancestors and Sibyls, including Augustus, who installed the Black-*Di-ana* as promised to the goddess. In many of the African lore that flourished in Asia Minor and all throughout Greece and Rome, the black (Egyptian) *Hercules* would often be equated with *Atlas* or with *Noah.*

Pope Declare s "Age of Apostles and Prophecy Over"
All Future African Prophetesses and Prophets Labeled
"*Frauds and Heretics*"

The Levitical Jews, just as the Muslim Arabs, both claim *Abraham*, whom was neither Arab nor Jew[95], as their divine ancestor. These Jews also claimed that their Hebrew prophets parallel those of the Sibyls. However, they do not answer why the Jews altered the prophecies of the Sibyls made from their *Omphaé* temple in Palestine, just to assure the hegemony of their fire god "*Yahweh/Jehovah,*" over the Christian "*Jesus.*" They plagiarized and published (in particular Sibylline Books III, IV and V) and widely circulated their own corrupted versions of these sacred Oracles in the name of Jehovah.[96]

We are told by Higgins, that the etymological root of "*Jehovah*", "*Ieue* or *Ieye*," had been deliberately disguised to conceal that it was an ancient praise word for *Krishna*. "IE" (jah) is also the symbol atop the Omphaé temple at Delphi and whose image was found in the ancient temple ruins at Thebes.[97] In other words, when this faction of Hebrews broke away from the Divine African Mother, they deliberately disguised their ancestral connection to Her and the Oannes, who have their ancient roots in actually in Ethiopian India. According to him, it was actually Krishna whom the Sibyls are said to come after Buddha, as the next incarnation of the "sun god."[98]

These Jews, further altered the oracles and placed into the mouths of their own prophets proclaiming themselves as the "*persecuted and chosen people*," for whom the Divine African Mother (now changed to "Yahweh/Jehovah") was referencing.

Roman theologian, Tertullian (c.160-c.230), even admits that :

"The Sibyl [prophecies] was Ancienter than all the Heathen Learning; that told real Events; and whose words you have put into the mouths of your prophets [instead of] the Demons.[99]

By this time, African deities were as a rule, referred to as the *Christianized "daemons/demons."* A Greek word, actually meaning "*spirit or familiar.*" More profoundly, what is being implied in the above, is an admission that the biblical books claimed to have been written by Hebrew prophets, may have actually been the prophecies of the Sibyls.

Overtime, being aware of the monumental task and near impossibility of removing all traces of the Sibyls from written history, the Jews in attempting to disguise the African, "*pagan/heathen*" origins of the Sibyls, delineated them as being of "*Persian*" (Aryan) descent and of the "*Zoroastrian order*".

However, when one considers the philosophy of *Zoroaster*, a fiercely nationalistic and virulent misogynistic, Iranian prophet, who hated women and predicted that most were doomed to "*go to hell*," one can appreciate the utter absurdity and recklessness of such a historic cover-up.[100]

The Roman Church, in their ignorance and ambition, acquired and doctored the Jews' corrupted versions, until one could hardly distinguish one forgery from the other. Not wanting to acknowledge the prophecies as being forged to establish the foundation of Christianity, the Christian papacy forbade the reading of the Bible entirely. Then, in an attempt at covering all of their bases, they historically documented the most famous of these Sibyls as being "*white*, "*virgin*", "*saved*"," *pure*"and"*Christ inspired*." Their "official" justification being:

This agitation of the Devils and the replies of the Idols lasted until the coming of Christ Our Lord, who brought the olive branch as a sign that the tempests of Idolatry has passed away. [101]

Nonetheless, though the Jews and Christians were feuding rivals, it was in both of their interest to suppress the prophetic power, influence and worship of the Divine African Mother. As a final act of apostasy, in their corrupted books, they both placed in the mouth of the Sibyls proclamations speaking against "*idolatry, serpent worship, initiations, polytheism, divination, sacrifice, astrology and astronomy.* In other words, the Sibyls were now preaching against the very source of their own divine authority(!). Moreover, they were contradicting all of the tenants and ritualistic functions of African and Chaldean religions, for which neither the Jews nor the Roman Church possessed any ecclesiastical authority, esoteric power, nor favor with the African deities.[102]

The church fathers did not stop there. In their revisionist fervor to justify the abrupt absence of no future Sibyl prophecies, since the death of Christ, these church fathers simply placed in the mouth of the *Erythraean* Sibyl the following proclamation:

"Why O Lord dost thou compel me still to foretell the future, and not rather remove me from this earth to await the blessed day of thy coming?"[103]

In other words, it was now time to suppress any further prophetic renderings for he [Christ] has already *"come and gone.,"* and it had already been written that he would *"rise again."* It was also time for the church fathers to create a separate and entirely different mythos for their verison of this "Christ," albeit, lifted whole cloth from the Egyptian mythos of Osiris.

Evangelistic Fever: In Search of the [African]Heathens

One century later, with the Roman church's power assured, the apostle Paul, armed with their corrupted theology, wasted no time in using the Church's propaganda against the multiracial inhabitants of Asia Minor (Turkey) and Greece (Corinth, Thessaly, Samos and Lydia). However, many of their earlier "evangelists" had already been duly slaughtered wholesale by the people, who knew the true history of their own gods. They also knew the Roman church's "prophetic" books to be corrupted forgeries of the original Sibyls, whose priestesshood, though suppressed ,was still strong in the remote villages.

The Africans and others rejected wholesale the naive notion of a *"virgin birth,"* an *"only begotten son,"* and an actual *"resurrection of the flesh."* Recognizing these as allegorical references to their traditional, sacrificial ceremonies of the sacred kings.

A deliberate, well organized campaign began to discredit, to persecute and to suppress any future utterances and divine powers or reactionary efforts on the part of the Sibyls and African priests who would not submit to the new church's doctrines. The church in their convoluted attempt to have it both ways, monopolized the writings and history of the Sibyls as white, but cursed them in public as *witches* and *demons*.

ENSLAVED, PERSECUTED PRIESTESS IN ROME

Fig 18: (rt) Frighten, Afro-Roman woman being sold into slavery against her will. In the utmost humiliation, her price and life history hangs around her neck. Western historical revisionists, and Hollywood have done a superb job in convincing the world that black Africa's predominance never existed outside of continental Africa. They have alleged that those Africans allowed "in-camera" have always been slaves or servants to a white, Roman aristocracy. However, just as ancient Greek history tell us that a black matriarchal presence first existed before the Dorian Greek arrival, the same holds true for Rome. Africans (black Buddhists Umbrians, and black Etruscans etc.,) erected civilizations in what is now Italy, thousands of years before the Anglo-Romans arrived. What is now called the "seat of the Vatican" in Italy, was originally the sacerdotal seat of the ancient black Sibyls. It was their thrones and sacerdotal power, and prophecies that was stolen from them, and their religions labeled as "pagan/heathen" under a racialist Roman Church. It was this African traditional religionist groups and not the so-called "Christians" who were the actual ones persecuted and finally enslaved as the above African woman, who was probably a priestess.

Fig 18: Enslaved and persecuted Afro-Roman priestess. The fall of the black matriarchal sacerdotal power around the world is a history that has never been told.

AFRICAN SACERDOTAL AUTHORITY AND TOTEMIC TRADITIONS UNDERMINED AND DEMONIZED UNDER EURO-CHRISTENDOM

Fig 19: "witch" consorting "black familiar." Europe 1621. British Mus.

Fig 19: (above)

It is no secret that the so-called "*Eleusinian Mysteries*" of Athens the Pythagorean mystery schools, and many other esoteric African spiritual paths that spread throughout Europe, were the cultural celebrations of Mami as "*De-meter, Cybelle and Ceres.*" During the European witch trials of the 15th-17th century, the Roman Imperial Church keenly aware of this, associated "*evil and demonology*" directly with the serpent worshiping Sibs of these African traditions. It was their votaries and the Sibyls that were the first to be persecuted as "witches." Though the early church fathers unashamedly consulted the "Pythias/Sibyls" for prophetic insight and military and, strategic direction when it was convenient for them, once they were done, they wasted no time in blaming them and their totems, as the center of spiritual corruption, social and moral decay, sexual promiscuity and evil in Europe. In the scene above the "black"' grotesque creature, is representing probably a Sibyl priestess with the ears of a bat and the legs of a goat and the tail of a donkey or dog, and the feet of a horse. The majority of the animals are the ancestral, totemic manifestations of the clans that these Sibs descend. Disparaging terms such as "black magic", "black arts," "necromancy", (from "nigromancy"), etc., were all euphemisms for any spiritual practices associated with Africa in general, and the Sibyls and their votaries in particular.

For example, the Cumean Sybil, *Herophile*, once worshiped and hailed by the Romans as a *"divine goddess"*, is now rewarded with a place in the Old Testament as the *"bat-Lady"* or the *"witch of Endor."* (Samuel 1: 28). The Divine Mother, (now masculinized as "father") was angered by his chasing the Sibyls (pythoness) out of the city. The Spirits refused to answer him by his own oracles, nor by dreams, nor by the *Urim* (Hebrew divination of throwing the knuckle bones of a ram as dice), nor by their Hebrew prophets."[104]

The Church papals were not finished. Because they now attributed all divine prophetic and healing powers only to "Christ," Herophile, being emblematical of the entire African religious tradition, was now demonized. In exposing the hypocrisy and sentiment of the Church, he sums it up in the following terms:

The first and most illustrious of witches-ancestor, mother, model, prototype, and flawless exemplar of all mediaeval witches–that venerable pythoness, the Witch of Endor . . . was a necromancer. Her special mastership lay in enforcing the appearance of the dead; we see in the fact that she had no difficulty in making the Prophet Samuel come out of his tomb. Power or no, he could not escape the dark power of that diabolical woman.[105]

Day of Doom: Final Prophecy for Rome

In the end, none of Rome's heroic efforts could stave off the inevitable fate of its impending destruction. In a desperate attempt to prevent the inevitable, the papal imperials searched desperately for the unfilled prophecies of the Sibyl's concerning Rome's final fate. Scrambling aimlessly through the Sibylline oracles, which had by now undergone a total masculinization and Christianization of "God," they tripped and stumbled upon a few verses, revealing that the die had already been cast. The Divine African Mother, who now delighted in prophesying their destruction, in her final words, had only this to say:

Thrice three hundred years having run their course of fulfillment,
Rome by the strife her people shall perish. . . . Rome is doomed to
perish, and that indeed by the judgement of God, because it held
H[er] name in hatred; and being the enemy of righteousness, it
destroyed the people who kept the truth."

There shall come to thee sometime from above
A heavenly stroke deserved, O haughty Rome.
And thou shalt be the first to bend they neck
And be rased to the ground, and thee shall fire
Destructive utterly consume, cast down
upon thy pavements, and thy wealth shall perish,
And wolves and foxes dwell in they foundations,
And then shalt thou be wholly desolate,
As if not born.[106]

The Final Fall and Dispersion

In the years following, specifically between *150 C.E-475 C.E*, Rome's population had increased, burden by heavy bureaucracy, and their patricians became lazy their bellies filled with the spoils of their colonial wealth. Its citizens were further weakened by numerous civil wars and devastating plagues. Rome was prime for the barbarian, Germanic invasions (Huns, Gauls) from the North, to which they eventually succumbed. The official cause of the young empire's collapse, was just simply an over burdened bureaucracy, moral decay and political corruption. However, beneath the substratum lies the story of the Sibyls, the African gods and the destiny of a forgotten people.

Fig. 19: Togolese Vodoun *Togbui/Amengansie*(chief elder) with ancestral python "oracular" serpent. The sacred ancestral python has its genesis in Africa, its people, and in their ancient spirituality; the oldest religions and unparallel sacerdotal mysteries in the world; especially in the Mami Wata tradition. Depending on the ancestral lineage, some priestesses and priests may display a literal serpent, but most Mami priestesses do not.

What became of the Sibyls?

In a final effort to blot out all traces of the ancient African matriarch's and later, the patriarch's undeniable presence and influence in the ancient world- one of the most egregious historical lies disseminated by the imperial Church in Rome, and continued unchallenged by present day Western historians, is their unproved claim that all of the descendants of the ancient black, *Egyptians, Phrygians, Pelasgian, Phoenicians/Canaanites and Syrians*, including their culture, religion and their languages, are now completely extinct. Western historians erroneously assert that these major African clans left no remote traces of themselves neither in Africa nor anywhere else in the world(!).

These "holy" papal fathers further designated the above ethnic classifications to the present day occupants of *Egypt, Greece, Turkey and Syria* respectively, misleading the entire world to believe that they are the actual descendants of the original indigenous African and Afro-Elamite groups whose powerful empires once ruled the ancient world.

One might well conjecture that the Africans, from all indications, during their persecution in Rome, may have already begun their sporadic migrations south westerly back into Africa, decades before the final fall of Rome. However, what is certain, is that as soon as they returned, they began empire building in West Africa. Albeit, employing the current oppressive, patriarchal model so often mistaken by cultural anthropologists as Africa's original indigenous culture. Many Africans until today, have on ikling that all of Africa was once ruled by their beloved matriarchs.

The Roman church and its imperialistic designs attempted/plotted to control all of the African continent. This hostile climate, aided by the church's financial backing, helped to create an atmosphere for chattel slavery and the ultimate colonization of all of Africa in the New World.

Though they were not alone in their determination to wipe out all traces of Africa's powerful religions, one of the first orders of the Christian missionaries commissioned by the church, was the complete and absolute destruction of Africa's temples , deities and shrines; as well as the total discrediting of Africa's priestshoods and knowledgeable elders, and the systematic removal of all African women from their sacerdotal roles. Further, the perpetual povertization of Africa created the perfect climate to impose an inferior and fictitious brand of Christianity such as what exist today throughout the continent. African and Diaspora families often bitterly divided between those who honor the old gods and customs established by their ancient mothers and fathers, and those who worship the colonial religion of Christianity introduced by the emissaries of the papal authorities.

The church's persecution did not stop there. Centuries later, backed by the church's blessings and money, millions of Africans were unwillingly transported across the great oceans and enslaved to lay the economic and cultural foundation of the *"New Rome"* in the Americas. An untold number of Africans in the New World are the blood descendants of those ancient *"serpent worshiping"* matrilineal descendants, long ago scattered throughout all four corners of the world, during the trans-Atlantic voyages. In the New World the demonization of both the African presence and their religions still continues unabated.

Today, few continental Africans or those in the Diaspora, hardly make the historic connection between the current status of African women and their ancient religions. Both having been relegated to an inferior status and a low economic and cultural priority by its fiercely patriarchal governments. Not to mention that only one country in all of Africa *Benin*, actually recognizes the ancient religion, *Vodoun*, established first by their ancient mothers (see chp 9), as its country's national religion.

The *Dogon, Ewe, Akan, Mossi, Mendes* and other African clans whom trace their ancient ancestral roots back to ancient *Nubia, Egypt, Ethiopia* and other ancient locations, still possess the knowledge of the sacred rites of which the church has never been successful at completely eradicating. In West Africa, the priestess-hoods of the Sibyls, now known as *Mammi/Mamisis/Mamaisis,"* (priestess of Isis), and those of the *Amengansies* (calling the dead), still continue unabated, within their *"serpent worshiping"* Sibs of the Yeveh Vodoun, and elsewhere.

Unfulfilled Prophecy in the West?

According to St. Augustine, it was Rome to whom the Sibyls referred as the true *"whore of Babylon."* In one final prophecy, believed yet to be fulfilled the Sibyls declares:

A great mischief shall befall Europe from the breed of Saturn, and the offspring of a spurious Servant; and they shall conquer strong Babylon: and when of all [the] countries which the sun shines on; she has been called Queen, she shall be destroyed by extraordinary ruin, and shall not give laws to her wandering Posterity [offspring].[107]

Considering today's political climate, one could speculate much from this and not render too far off target. However, what is most important here for the African Diaspora, as the benefactor of the divine seed of their gods and ancestors is that whatever belies the fate of the world, in spite of how Western biblical prophecy has been perverted and corrupted to disguise or exclude African people and others, it is important for them to reconnect back with their own divine self with the utmost expediency.

By removing the antiquated shackles of mental slavery, the accompanying psychological fear and ignorance, only then will they begin the important work of restoring the dignity and the respect for their African Spirits and Ancestors that are *cosmo* and *biogenetically* linked to them. Accomplishing this could prove not only beneficial to the world at large, but also might be the greatest cultural, political and spiritual triumph of all time.

NOTES

1. Higgins, Vol. I. p. 615, 627-628.;Temple, p. 181 ("first fruits". Still performed as "Agbandoto" in Togo, and by Mami Wata Healing Society in Augusta, GA).

2. Hyatt M. H. "Hoodoo-Conjuration-Witchcraft-Rootwork" (Illinois: Alama Egan Hyatt Foundation, 1973), Vols. I-V. p. I.

3. Ibid.

4. Ciholas, p. 162.

5. Neuman, p. 135-136.; Smith, p. 58.

6. The History of Herodotus, 440 B.C.EE., Book V.; see also Temple p. 194

7. Ibid.

8. Temple, p. 195.

9. Higgins, Vol 2., p. 328, Vol I. p. n.591.

10. Monterio, p. 159.;Graves, Greek Myths 1. p. 18.3.

11.Ibid. p. 75.; Bell. p. 204.; Tyndal. I Sam: 28.;Ciholas. p. 129.;Webster's II. p. 642.;Webster's New Collegiate Dictionary. P. 1077 (see also: The Oxford Compact Dictionary. Oxford University Press. Second Edition, 2003.

12. Ibid.;Ciholas, Paul. The Omphalos and the Cross: Pagans and Christians in Search of a Divine Center. Macon: Mercer University Press, 2003. p. 123;132.

13. Higgins, Vol I. p. 189,422,585,599.;Ciholas, p. 127,132-133n.11,154.;Lederer, p.151,152.

14. Graves, Greek Myths 1. p. 105.; Monterio, p.150.;Bell 130. The Sibyls shines and temples were located all throughout the known world, including Kemet (Egypt), Libya, Greece, Sparta, Persia, Peloponnesus (Turkey) the Minoan and Ionian Islands, Rome etc.,.

15. see note 6

16. Monteiro, p. 161; Stone 112.

17. The word "Garmantes" is also a variation of "Coromanti and Kormantin, Gourmantché," which are English and Dutch equivalents, referring to the now present day Guan, Ga-Adangbe clans of N. Ghana and the Anlo-Ewe near Elmina, and the Gur groups of Burkino Faso. Dr.J.D. Elder. African Survivals. p. 15.; Encyclopedia Brit. Micro. Vol. III. 1976, p. 455-456.;Graves, The Greek Myths, I. p. 45. pottery shards date the black Libyan arrival as early as 4,000 B.C.E; The White Goddes. p. 177.; Temple, p. 244. Black, matriarchal clans were already in an advance stage of civilization 3000 years before the arrival and cultural assimilation of the Dorian (mixed-race) Greeks, Persians and Turks. Jealousy of these black matriarchs power and prosperity is what prompted the patriarchal invasions.;Briffault, p. 66,66. Although Briffault has made the same mistake as earlier researchers in classifying the ancient North Africans and Libyans as "white," he does make their connection to the Mycenaean cultures of Asia Minor.

18. Webster's New Collegiate Dictionary, 1977, p. 1076.

19. Ibid. Temple, p. 174.

20. Briffault, p. 103.

21. Diner, Helen. "Mothers and Amazons: The First Feminine History of Culture."(New York: Double Day Anchor Press, 1973. p. 192,190-191.

22. Horton, p. 224-232.; Ibid. Encyclopedia Brit. Micro. Vol. VIII. 1976, p. 892-893.;Graves, The White Goddess," p. 447.; Sappho, known since antiquity to have been the single major influence on Western poetry and literature, inspiring the

works of *Tennyson* and others, was hailed as the *"Queen of Poetry."* Sappho," was born on the Greek Island of *Lesbos* (Levsos), in the town of *Eresus* (610-c. 580 B.C.E). However, she actually grew-up in *Mitylene*. Described as a *"small, dark body filled with immortal fire,"* she wrote her name in her own Afro-Aeolic dialect as *"Psappho."* She was considered the greatest literary poetess of her time, and some have even argued *"of all ages."* She spoke and wrote in the native Aeolian dialect, and her poetry was written in what would be called today, a *"street vernacular style."* Born from an aristocratic family, this black, educated women enjoyed "hanging out" with the ladies on the island of Lesbos, holding poetry circles, that she founded. Although Psappho was married (Cercylas) and had birthed a daughter (Cleis), her poetry centered on intense erotic amours with other women. In her poetry she also expressed her fears, hatred and jealousies just as equally against her rivals and enemies. During the Middle Ages, the books that survived the Inquisitions, were completely destroyed. Only quotes of two long poems, and few single-line fragments have been preserved. In spite of Graves resentment of the *"Attic comedians who caricature her as an insatiable Lesbian,"* Psappho is still hailed as a s/hero to the black lesbian communities, and to others, who view her as an exemplar during a time when the barbarity of Christian patriarchy had concealed and destroyed their S/heros.

23. Horton, George. *Home of the Nymphs & Vampires: The Isles of Greece.* Indianapolis:Bobbs-Merrill Company, 1929, p. 282-283.
Higgins, p. 435.;*Encyclopedia Brit. Micro. Vol. V. 1976, p. 410-411.*
24. Ibid. p. 259.; Higgins, p. 456, Rhodes was one of ten islands known collectively as "the *Dodecanese*." (a Greek word "dodeka and nesos", meaning *ten islands*).After the patriarchal incursion, it was later known as *the "Bride of the Sun,* and "Land of the Roses." The sun was said to be named after the black Egyptian *"Cercaphos,"* who was the *"daughter of the Sun."*
25. Horton, p. 86.
26. Ibid. p. 87.
27. Ibid. p. 86
28. Ibid. p. 88.
29. *Horton, p. 88,282.;Encyclopedia Brit. Micro. Vol. III. 1976, p. 451-452;.* Bell, p. 127-30. Higgins, Vol I. p. 227.
31.Higgins, Vol I. p. 709.
32. Brown JNR., p. 78,Higgins, p. Vol I. p. 364, 702, Vol II. p. 768-769
33. Diner, p. 188-190.; see Bibliography for "on-line notes" *'Lycian Turkey: The Federalist Papers'.;*Osei, Osafo. K. *"A Discourse on Akan Perpetual Calendar."* Accra: Ghana, 199, p. xiii.
34. Ibid.
35. Ibid., p. 188.
36. *Encyclopedia Brit. Micro. Vol. V. 1976, p. 706-707.;*Smith, p. 41.
37. Bulwer-Lytton. Sir Eward, Bart. *"The Last Days of Pompeii."* London: A.L. Burt Company, Publishers, 1850, p. 207.
38. Ibid, p. 58; Bell, p. 247.
39. Monteiro, p. 24,75.;Higgins, p. 812-813.
40. Lederer, p.151,152.;Ciholas, p. 127,133-134,138,140, 157.

41.13. Monterio, p. 16-17.; Bell Vol. II, p.121.;Graves, *I Claudius*.

42 Lederer, p. 170-171.; Frazer, p. 348.; Higgins, Vol. I. p. 137.;Encyclopedia Britannica. Micropaedia. Ready Reference. 15th ed., 1974, Vol. I. p.649.

43. Bell, Vol. II. p. 121.

44. Ibid., 121.

45. Ciholas, p. 142, 136

46 Herodotus, Book V.;Graves. Greek Myths. Vol 2, p.162.

47. Ibid. p. 150.

48. Ibid. 153.

49. *"The Living Bible Paraphrased."* Wheaton: Tyndall House Publishers Inc., 1971. I Sam. 28:6; 28:13. DiGivry, p. 167.; Lederer, p.151.; Frazer. p. 3.; Ciholas. p. 127,161.

50. Monterio, p. 84,172.

51. Ibid., 136.

52. Bell, p. Vol II. 122.

53.Stone, p.55,165-166.; Lederer, p. 157,159,169.;Graves, Greek Myths 2. p.190.;Walker, p.30-31.

54. *Encyclopedia Brit. Micro. Vol. III. 1976, p. 455-456.;Graves*, The Greek Myths, I. p. 45. ; *The White Goddes. p. 177.;* Temple, p. 244..;*Briffault, p. 66,66.*

55.Walker, p. 46-47.

56. Ciholas,p.131.: Terry,Vol. III. p. 1023-31.

57. Ciholas, p. 123, 125.; Lederer, p. 149, 152, 158-159.

58. Terry, Milton. S. *The Sibylline Oracles.* Translated From the Greek into English Black Verse. New York: Eaton & Mains, 1899.;Monteiro, M., White, A.C. *As David and the Sibyls Say.* Montana: Kessinger,1905.;Graves, Robert. *"The White Goddess." Amended and Enlarged Edition.*(New York: Farrar, Strass, and Giroux,1980), p105,228, 254.;Higgins,Vol.I,167,427,519,540,563-566,574,613,634-637,663,666,671.;Bell, John. Bell's *New Pantheon or Historical Dictionary of the Gods, Demi Gods, Heroes and Fabulous Personages of Antiquity* Vol. I. II. London: British Library, Strand, 1790, p.234-237.;Stone, Merlin. *"When God Was A Woman"* (New York: Barnes & Noble Books, 1993), p. 211.;Frazer, James, G. Sir. *"The Golden Bough: A study in magic and religion"* (New York: The Macmillan Co., 1943), Vol I., p. 3,348.;Temple, Robert. *"The Sirius Mystery"* (United Kingdom: Arrow Pub., 1999), p. 172,178, 194-195.

59. Monteiro. p. 40.

60. Ibid. p.100.

61. Ibid.

62. Graves, Greek Myths, Vol 2. p. 131.; (see also *"Gargars"* link in On-Line Resources,).

63.Stone, p.55,165-166.; Lederer, p. 157,159,169.;Graves, Greek Myths 2. p. 190.;Walker, p.30-31.

64. Ibid. p. 73.

65. Graves, *Greek Myths*, p. 28-29.;Monteiro, p. 73.Graves, *White Goddess*, p. 336.

66. Monterio. p. 160-161, 164-165.

67.Neuman,p.218.;Higgins,p.264,332,333,456.;Stone,p.88-93, 151,204-205.;207-211.;Walker,p.502-503.;Graves,Greek Myths 1. p. 28.2,31c,32.1,33,35.5,38.1 &38.4, 45,47.131.2,131.4,135.3; Graves. The White Goddess, p. 316,356.

68. Bell, p. 135.

69. Ciholas, p. 131.; Graves, Vol I.p. 51. 53

70. Lederer, p. 149.; Bell, p. 177.; Graves, p. 390.

71. Monteiro, p. 9.
72. Ibid. p. 9-10.
73. Monteiro, p. 6.
74. Tirmizi, p. 1.
75. Bell, p.95.
76 .Monterio. p 154.
77. Monteiro, p. 161, 148, 24, 91.
78. Monteiro, p. 25,27.: Bell 235.
79. Graves. *I Claudius*, p. 6.
80. Smith, p. 37.
81. Monteiro, p. 160-161.
82. Clifton, p.98-99
83. Ibid: Encycl. Brit. Vol VI, p. 1012-13.
84. Ibid. p. 191.
85. Bell. p. 124-125,235-237.
86. Temple,p.237.: Waljer, p. E.W.S., p. 208.
87. Ciholas, p. 125-126.:Bell, p.124-125.:Walker, p. 208.
88. Temple, p. 237.
89. Higgins, Vol I. p. 190.
90.Bell. p. 236.
91. Monterio. p. 12.
92. Monterio, p. 44 : Bell, p. 236.: Ciholas, p. 134,137.
93. Ciholas, p. 138.
94. Ibid. p. 139.
95. Abraham was a diviner and Shepard from the black, East African clan of the *Korites*, meaning worshipers of Isis in her grain and fecundity aspect as the goddess Kore. Mohammed built his tradition from these long established black, matriarchal worshipers of the black goddess *Al-lat (Awussa)*, who have now been reduced to his *"daughters."*
96. Hammer, p. 61.
97. Higgings, Vol I. p. 59, 243,586.
98.Ibid. p. 158-159,253,429.
99. Monteiro, p. 99.
100. Ciholas, p. 1146-47, 150.;Walker, p. 1102.; Barnstone, p. 501-502,555-561.
101. Monteiro. p. 11. 13.
102. Ciholas, p. 162
103. Ibid.
104. Lederer, p. 151.
105. DeGivry, p. 167.
106. Ciholas, p. 140-141.
107.Monteiro. p. 103.

IMAGES OF ANCIENT SIBYLS

BLACK CHALDEANS: WORLD'S FIRST MASTER ASTRONOMER'S

"I admit with great difficulty the theory of all early astronomical knowledge of the Chaldees having been acquired or invented by this race, and that the Chaldees were originally Negroes. But this prejudice wears away when I go to the precursors of the Brahmins, the Buddhists, and when I reflect upon the skill in the fine arts which they must have possessed when they executed the beautiful and most ancient sculptures in the Museums of the India-house, and the knowledge of astronomy shewn in their cycles of stones." Higgins, *Anacalypsis* Vol. II. p. 364.

Fig 20: Black Chaldean Priest: Above, is an astronomical chart reflecting the microcosm and celestial worlds, The black Egyptian pyramid surrounded by the holy nimbus (halo) at the top, is actually based on an ancient cone pillar (*womb/omphaé*), one of the primeval symbols of *Isis* and *Black Di-Ana*. One of the above names "*Epiphania*" (rt. top) describes one of the oldest settlements of the black, matriarchal, Chaldean and *Canaanite clans* in ancient Syria. Originally named *Oiniandos by them*, they had occupied it since prehistoric times; including during the Hattie empire which they founded. In the 9th century, they were invaded by the Assyrians, and many fled to Asia Minor (now Turkey) and founded a settlement bearing the same name, located near the ancient Ethiopian, *Mattani* empire. The name "*Epiphania*" was later given to the province by *Seleucid*, one of Alexander "*The Great*" generals, who defeated the Assyrians, and became king of the region after Alexander's death in 323 B.C.E. *Epiphania* also appears to be a corruption of *Epiphany*, an ancient word later borrowed by the Christians, but originally meant to describe the ceremonial night vigils held by the masses to witness the literal spirit manifestation of the black goddesses, and gods, especially *Isis, Osiris*, Ceres and *Black Di-Ana*.

An African Divine History Hidden and Obscured in Time

During ancient times, it was the Chaldean priests who manifested materially and mystically the desires of the African Gods. They came originally out of ancient *Egypt, Nubia, Ethiopia, Syria, Persia*, and made their way into Ionia, Asia Minor, and India. Initiated into the mysteries of Mami and the *Dionysus/Bacchus (Osiris)* orders, these African men were master astronomers, astrologers, prophets, alchemists (Magi), and masons (architectural engineers). Just as the Sibyls, these priests were the early inventors and masters of nearly all forms of divination, including *"augury"* (messenger by birds) and *ventriloquism, tarot, cards, bones, dice etc.,*. These master priests prepared the solar calendars, and were the interpreters of dreams, and visions in the royal court of Kings. The Ethiopian prophet *Abraham/Abram*, (who was neither Arab or Jew), was head of the Chaldean order of diviners, just as his father who made his living constructing votive images of *Kore/Black Di-Ana* once was.

The Chaldean priests (meaning *"moon mother"*) honored the Divine African Mother, and worked together with the Sibyls in establishing the ancestral shrines *"omphalé"* throughout the ancient world. Most of the original architectural designs of Mycenae, Ionia, and Aegean islands attributed to the Greeks, was actually built by these priests and the *Chaldæi* (black Amazons). Once those temples were destroyed, the Greeks (and later the Romans) simply rebuilt them copying the same architectural designs, but *Anglozing* the sacred images of the gods and goddesses.

As master mathematicians, the Chaldeans were the primary forecasters and validators of astronomical events, and divine cycles relating to prophecy as foretold by the Sibyls. In ancient Egypt, their most oldest predecessors were known as the *"Ketui"* (Ewe"*Kettas"*) or *"stone builders"* who were later called the *"Morions,"*by the European Bards, because they were jet, black like the smoked quartz which bears the same name. However, the name is also a term used for calculating and predicting the motions of spaceships and other heavenly bodies, because the European *Bards* (minstrel-poets) who would often baffoon them in black-face, also knew them and the Amazons to be the actual builders of the ancient, Buddhists mega-structures known as *Stonehenge'*. It was believed to have been an observatory location for monitoring certain celestial events.

During those times, as the above Roman chart indicates, it was common knowledge that the ancient *Chaldean* priests were originally African. As initiates of the goddesses of *Fate* and *Destiny*, equal to their contemporary *Gabadu*", in the Mami Vodoun Afa system of divination, it was through *their* permission upon entering into *their* mysteries that the ancient Chaldean diviners received their divinatory, and magical powers.

NOTES:

1. Massey, The Book of the Beginnings, p.218,; Higgins, Vol 1. p. 311,513,;Smith, G. *"Chaldean Account of Genesis.*

ANCIENT AKKADIANS (AKANS) OF BABYLON

Fig 21: A Forester's recreation (based on archeological evidence) of ceremonial sacrifices at the Kings Grave in ancient Ur (Babylon). Black Akkadians (Akkad="*serpent worshipers*") covered in sacred white kaolin, the color of death or "spirit." It is from these ancient groups that the Chaldean Sibyl descends. It is also from these groups where the main manufacturing of the sacred heavily, ornamented veil draped across the holy images of Isis, and the Black Di-Ana of Ephesus were constructed.   British Museum, 1928.

SIBYL QUEEN MOTHERS IN ANCIENT HISTORY

Fig 22: Sibyl queen mother, triple-crowned, as Black Dio-Ana. She was worshiped as triple-headed Janus in Rome. The double-coiled scarf representing the twin serpents of Mami.

Fig 23: Sibyl prophetess on Moors coat-of-arms. No miliary leader would conduct tactical operations without first consulting a Sibyl and making the necessary propitiations to Mami and the ancestors. Long before the use of European "Saints", images of Mami or a Sibyl was worn on coat-of-arms or hung outside of businesses for protection and good-luck.

Fig 24: Sibyl queen on Moor Coat of Arms, wearing six-pointed crown of Mami-Tanit. All African Queens were Sibyls, but not all Sibyls were queens or prophetess.

CHALDEAN SIBYL ON SISTINE CHAPEL

Fig 25: Enlargment of black, Chaldean (Persian), Sibyl Prophetess, *Sambeth*, holding her book of prophecy   Sistine Chapel, Rome.

Fig 26: Below, Michelangelo's phantasy of black, Chaldean (Persian) Sibyl Prophetess, *Sambeth*, assigned a meager place in corner (arrow, bottom right), while the white female image is assumed to be her. The systematic misrepresentation of black god/desses, and heros as "*white*" was a gradual, and subtle process, until Europe's supremacy was assured. Then, all black images were reproduced as white, or reclassified as "slaves," or their images and history destroyed entirely.   Painted on Sistine Chapel, Rome.

LIBYAN SIBYL ON SISTINE CHAPEL

Fig 27: Enlargement of black, Libyan, Sibyl
Prophetess, *Bybissa*, with perhaps another Sibyl
in draped in a white African wrap.   Sistine
Chapel, Rome.

Fig 28: Below, Michelangelo's phantasy of black, Libyan, Sibyl Prophetess,
Bybissa, assigned a meager place in corner (arrow, mid-lleft), while the white
female image holding *Bybissa's* book of prophecies is assumed to be her.

DELPHI SIBYL ON SISTINE CHAPEL

Fig 29: Enlargement of Delphic, Sibyl
prophetess, *Themis*, from below.
Sistine Chapel, Rome.

Fig 30: Below, Michelangelo's phantasy and out right misrepresentation of the
Delphic, Sibyl prophetess, *Themis*, as a white woman. Conversely, he has
assigned a meager place in the back to the authentic *"black dove."* (arrow,
center).

"ROMANIZED" SIBYL ON POPE'S TOMB

Fig 31: Roman model posing as
Ethiopian/ "Phrygian Sibyl" on the tomb
of Pope Hadrian IV. Rome. 1524 and
1529

Fig 31: Above, Roman, model posing as black, "Ethiopian/Phrygian Sibyl" on the tomb
of Pope Hadrian IV. (C.E. 117-138). Claimed to be the last of the "non-Italian" popes
before John Paul II, it was Hadrian, a black, Phrygian from Thrace (now, N. E. Greece)
who set the literary, cultural and religious style of Rome during that time period.[1] It was
considered fashionable for Popes, Emperors, Patricians, and dignitaries to claim an
African, divine, maternal linage from the Serpent Spirit, and the Phrygian Sibyl *"Phrigia,"*
exemplified this. It was even believed that *Hadrian, Augustus,* and all twelve Caesars,
adopted their names, and calculated their reigns, based upon the Sibyl's prophecies.[2]
They believed the Neros would be the period in which the Messiah would come.[3] So
committed was Pope Hadrian that, as Emperor, he sent for a tutelary, African ancestral
Serpent to be ceremoniously placed in the Temple of Jupiter[4].   Hadrian, later wrote to
a friend

*"Those who worship Serapis [oracular, ancestral serpent] are also Christians; even those
who style themselves the Bishops of Christ are devoted to Serapis."*[5]

It was especially during Hadrian's reign that the divine Serapis was worshiped, sitting,
in full implements and regalia, on his throne, with Isis standing next to him; holding
her sacred Sistrum, in one hand and a sheaf of wheat in the other. Beneath them read
the inscription *"Immaculate is our Lady Isis,"* which of course, was later attributed to the
new image of her, made-over as the *"white, Virgin Mary."*[6]

Though modern, Western history has tried to conceal or deny an African world,
predominance in ancienr Greece and Rome, the trail of African deities, and their
specific, and unique bio-ancestral characteristics reveals another story.   (cont)

(cont)

African, and Afro-Phrygian, Afro-Judaic *(Ophites/Ophis/Cushite)*, Afro-Pelasgian, Afro-Byzantium, Afro-Etruscan, Afro-Umbrian, and Afro-Greco religions, and culture was already dominate in Italy, long before the formation of the Roman Empire. However, white models became common practice, under imperial Rome, when the Church had fully formulated a European religious and racial identity. During the Classical (actually "revisionist") era, they began to commission artists to replace the Sibyls, the Black Madonnas, and other African god/desses, thus, implying a European antiquity that simply *did not exist*. It is these deliberate, misrepresentations that have been passed down to the world today as "world *history*".

Santa Maria dell'Anima. Baldassare Peruzzi. 1524 and 1529

1. Encyclopedia Brit., Micropeadia, Vol. IV., 1973, p. 830.;Könemann, p. 431.
2. Higgins, Vol. I., p. 625, 613.
3. Ibid.
4. Forlong, p. 96.
5. Ibid. P. 510.
6. Ibid.

ROMANIZED "SIBYL PRIESTESS"

Fig 32: Roman model posing as black, Pythian
priestess, on tomb of Pope Sixtus IV (1414- 1484). She is
included as one of *"seven divine virtues,"*
Bronze, made by Antonio and Piero Pollaiuolo
(between 1484-1493), Rome

SIBYL IN WEST GERMAN BISHOP'S PALACE

Fig 33: Nubian Sibyl priestess resting on camel, painted on mural in Prince Bishop's Palace built around 1720-1744, in Wurzburg, Germany. During ancient times it was customary to parade the black goddesses in chariots, driven by mules, bulls, or oxen, or to display them riding atop the back of mules, camels and donkeys Paintings of the Sibyls in the Christian churches was considered critical in order to add an air of divine legitimacy to the bishop's authority. Many tourists who view these images today, have little or very scant knowledge of their original historic meaning. Photo © Mamaissii Vivian Hunter-Hindrew, 1992.

DAPHNE TREE
ANCESTRAL HOLY HERB OF THE SIBYLS

Monastery of a Sibyl at Daphne ("*sacred to sun* "). Once a sacred, it was destroyed in the 6th century and a church dedicated to the "Virgin."

Fig 34: Above, named after a location in ancient Egypt, the Taphnai or Daphne tree, (meaning *"sacred to the sun"*), was later known as the *bay laurel.* It was holy to Mami, and represented her sun consort. It was chewed by her initiated priestesses, especially the Sibyls," The Cumean Sybil (in Rome) was said to have written her nine books of prophecy on bay laurel leaves, and placed them in front of her shrine for the spirits to scatter them into the order of prediction. As with most consecrated shrines in Africa, this temple is probably where all initiations healings, divinations, rites of passage, ancestral ceremonies and other African rituals took place. Most of the ancient temples to the African goddesses were siezed, desecrated, pillaged, and its structure converted into Christian churches, along with its customs and rituals incorporated into Christian rites

SIBYLS REPRESENTING THE "FOUR SEASONS" IN ANCIENT ROME

Fig 35: Above, a Romanized verison of the four Sibyls representing the "Four Seasons," situated above the high altar, in a place of honor at the Imperial Palace in Ostia. Ostia, is a western, Roman city situated at the opening of the Tiber River. It is where several temples and mystery schools to Isis can be found buried. On the other side of the arch, are figures of Augustus, and the Tiburtine Sibyl. During Christmas, exhibitions of wooden figures are displayed depicting the Sibyl pointing out to Augustus the Black Virgin and the *Bambino* (black Madonna and Child), who appeared in the sky in a halo of light. These wooden images would occupy the front row for all to admire. They have since been hidden and eventually sold, (by a prince Alexander Torlonia, Lancini, p. 24-25), and are now replaced with a white Mary and Child. It is suggested that current church Papal authorities used the story told by Augustus as the basis for determining the authenticity of popular claims of "visitations" by Mary. Though they have succeeded in removing her and the Sibyls black images from the world's cathedrals, they remain very much aware of their true African "pagan" heritage.

EUROPEAN MOTIFS OF SIBYL PRIESTESSES

Above, examples of motif plates representing the Black Mami god/dess "Di-Ana." For centuries, European women graced their clothes, and vanity furniture with these African images as the symbol of wisdom and sensuality.

EUROPEAN MOTIF OF SIBYL PROPHETESS

CHRISTIAN MOTIF OF ST. MICHEAL MURDERING A BLACK SIBYL PROPHETESS

SIBYL DOLL BURIED IN ROME?

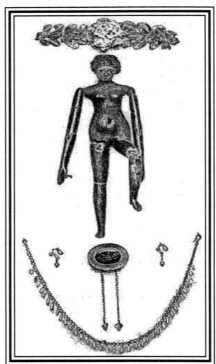

Fig 36: Black doll found in "pagan grave". Rome, (C.E. 193-211).

Fig 36: Above, black oak wood doll, found buried with a young girl, along with other objects found in a Roman, "*pagan cemetery*." She may have been a young Mami (Sibyl?) priestess. Her name was, *Crepereia Tryphaena*, and she lived during the reign of the Libyan, (Roman) Emperor, Septmius Lucius Severus (AD 193-211). No one knows her African name because it was said that she belonged to "*a family of freeman,*" who were former servants of a noble family named "*Creperei*". (her "enslaved name"). They believed that she was to be married that day, because she was found dressed in a white bridal gown, adorned with the jewelry (rubies and pearls) including two gold rings, one engraved with whom they believe to be her husband. Above her head is the bay laurel reef, worn by Sibyls and sacred to Mami and Apollo. In the sarcophagus, she is found in full bridal attire, her body and face covered in a white linen blanket, surrounded by other fine fabrics. The black doll was also dressed in bridal attire, and in its hand were two gold key rings. It was the custom for anyone (but required for initiates) to offer these dolls as a votive offering to Mami on ones wedding day. They said she died of *scrofula*, a tuberculous infection of the skin and neck. However, there is no evidence of this. She might simply have been taken by Mami, who might have preferred that she not marry.

BLACK SIBYLS *EUROPEANIZED* AND CONCEALED AS *"CHRISTIANS"*

Fig 37: Keeping in mind that their prophecies were made more than 3,000 years before Christ, and none of the Church fathers had ever met a Sibyl, the attire that these woman are adorned, is not the traditional dress that the ancient African Sibyls wore. The Sibyls, were the chief priestesses of an African divine matriarchal order. Completely demonized and forgotten by the Church papal, and Levtical Jewish priests, who exploited and desecrated their ancient prophecies, They have been immortalized as *European* by famous painters across Europe, including Castagno,.Von, Steinle, Cavaliere, Matteo da Sienna and Peruzzi, However, the most famous of these paintings are those by Michelangelo, at the Sistine Chapel. The first five originally depicted them situated alongside the Christian prophets. Until today, Africans and the world, remain unaware of who they are, and that they were not European saints, nor were they martyrs of a patriarchal, Euro-Western, Christian or Judaic doctrine.

CUMEAN "BAT" SIBYL

The Ancient African Tradition *of Calling-up the Dead*

Fig 38: "Bat Sibyl"

Fig 38: Above, featured on a Moors coat-of-arms, this "bat lady," is none other than the *Cumean Sybil, Herophile,* or one of her predecessors. They probably acquired the name *"bat Sibyl"*, because the totemic symbol of the bat signifies the gentle, unobtrusive, civil and shrewd character of this path of the Sybils, rather than the stereotypic "dark maleficent" nature black priestesses would later acquire. It was also the symbol of one who could call up and speak to the spirits of the dead, such as the ancient tradition of *Amengansies,* and certain Mamaissiis in the Mami Wata tradition in West Africa. During ancient times, the Sibyl would take the blood of a sacrificed bull, and mixed it with a secret beverage that they drank, to induce trance possession. This was simply one of many ways in which possession was achieved. During these ecstatic trance states, the Sibyls would either *"roll about on the ground [in full possession], or march back and forth, uttering prophetic prose"*, in what became infamously known as the *"eerie voice of a bat."* (Graves, W.G., p. 105). The shrine of the *Cumean Sybil* was located in a volcanic rock depression, beside Lake Avernus in Cumae, Rome and surrounded by oak and the black poplar trees sacred to Mami and the solar son/gods. It was at these brackish waters, where they would perform ceremonies to bring forth the spirits of the dead. It was one of these type Sibyls whom the biblical Saul went to in the town of Endor, disguised, and begging her to call up the spirit of the priest Samuel, after he had earlier just ordered all *"mediums and wizards out of the city."* (Sam 28:5-9). It is perhaps also from these divine women, that the word *necromancy* (originally *"nigromancy"*) was initially introduced. It later became exclusively employed to refer to anyone practicing the mystical and magical arts of African and Afro-Elamitic people. Racist epithets, such as *"black magic, trickery, wizardry, sorcerer, witchcraft,* and *evil spirits,"* were pejorative labels later employed to describe any African based religious system. Thus, it is no surprise that during Medieval Rome, the Sibyls (not white witches) were the *first* to be accused of "witchcraft, and of *uttering the voices of demons"*. They were the first to be burned at the stake, and the black Chaldean priests literally crucified for" *heresy and witchcraft."* They possessed the spiritual power, and ancient, mystical knowledge that could expose the fraudulent theology of the Church. They were, therefore, the biggest threat to the papacy, who possessed no divine lineage or authority, and thus could never perform the *"miracles of the spirit,"* as did these black clergy. However, today these special priestesses are called **"Amengansie"**, and the tradition of their ancient mothers of *"calling up the spirits of the dead,"* and other divinities is still extant in the Vodoun and Mami Wata religions in West Africa and in the Diaspora.

SIBYL "SORCERESS"

Figure 39: 7 B.C.? Mosaic entitled "*Women Consulting Sorceress.*" The women are wearing masks, according to museum description. However, their faces appear to be covered in the African traditional white "Ahliya," (kaolin). The "sorceress," is clearly a Sybil, depicted in usual "gorgon"style, as the "old black hag." It is interesting to note that the old English word for "*hag,*" is "*serpent*" (Hig. P. 518). In Mami Wata Vodoun, a queen priestess over fifty is honored, feared, and respected with the title of "*Akovi*". Above, she holds the sacred wine and maize beverage. This beverage was served in a silver chalice, and drank to induce trance possession by *some* pythian priestesses. Notice also the legendary bay laurel garland on the table. Sacred to Mami, and eaten before performing divination. Similar rites, are still performed in Vodoun and other African branches. These kinds of paintings were as much political as they were racist. After the Roman conquest of Pompeii, Rome continued their campaign of discrediting the black "pagan" traditions and replacing it with Christianity. However, the Romans were very much "pagan" and secretly enjoyed and participated in many African religious festivities. Pompeii, Villa of Cicero Naples, National Archaeological Museum. (Pg. 74).

It was widely rumored that it was actually the Sibyls who invented the alphabet. This was achieved, legend has it, by them writing down the prophetic voices that they heard onto laurel or palm leaves, while in a semi, self-induced trance. So widespread was this belief that Roman poet, Virgil (70-19 B.C.E), hailed as one of Rome's greatest poets, immortalized it into poem (below).

Virgil's Ode to the Sybil of Cumae

Arrived at Cumae, when you view the flood of black Avernus, and the sounding wood, The mad and prophetic Sybil you shall find Dark in a cave and on a rock reclined. She sings the fates, and in her frantic fits The notes and name inscribed TO LEAVES COMMITS

What she commits to leaves, in order laid, Before the carven's entrance are display'd. Unmoved they lie: but if a blast of wind Without or vapors issue from behind, The leaves are born aloft in liquid air; And she resumes no more her liquid care, Nor gather from the rocks her scatter'd verse, Nor sets in order what the winds disperse. Thus many not succeeding, most upbraid,The madness of the visionary maid. And with loud curses, leave the mystic shade.

Aen, Lib. III. Ver. 445

THE "UNHOLY" AFRICAN MOTHER?
(THE PAPAL WARS AGAINST MAMI-ISIS AND THE MYSTICAL POWER OF AFRICAN WOMEN)

Fig 40: (lt) this Sibyl, demonized by the Church as "Eve" can be found "copulating with a serpent," on the Church arch of *Oo*, located in Haute Garonne, a region of France. Degrading images such as these were displayed at more than sixty churches throughout France and were actually pre-emptive strikes against their powerful rival African temples of Mami-Isis, whom the people were more devoted. The war waged for the destruction of African and African influenced mystery schools by the growing Roman authorities was met with great resistance throughout the world.

Toulouse Museum.

B y the 1500 and 1600s, the war on African religious culture and clergy continued to be an important central target of Vatican authorities. Its primary aim was not only to colonize, and to pillage Africa, but also to destroy and obscure the direct ethnological, theological, cultural, and linguistic link to their own sacerdotal knowledge, which they knew originated in Africa. The divine, Serpent deity was central to African matriarchal, oracular tradition. It not being indigenous to European culture, only served to further perpetuate and to make believable the fantastical lies and myths of bizarre orgies, dark rituals and African debauchery perpetuated by the Church.

Overtime, all of Europe began to formulate a "*white*" racial identity based upon specific phenotypic (outer physical) characteristics. One of the indicators of "pure" Aryan blood was not to possess a lineage of any "*Taurian*" (meaning "black") blood in ones vein. The "*Taurians*" in Europe were identified as those "*serpent worshipers*" who introduced the Mami-Isis tradition in to Rome and Ireland. So connected were the nagas (serpent worshipers) with the "colored" races, that it became almost the exclusive litmus test for "Aryan purity". So prejudiced were they against them that in 1865, James Fergusson, Esq., in his research on serpent worship, comments that:

"We have not in Germany, as we find in Greece any traces of that underlying race of less intellectual Turanians who seem everywhere to have been the Serpent worshipers all the world over. Fergusson, James, Esq., F.R.S., M.R.A.S. *Tree and Serpent Worship: Illustrations of myth and art in India in the first and fourth centuries after Christ*" (London: India Museum of London, 1868), p. 20.

The European peasantry, by now in utter ignorance were just recovering from the *Dark Ages*. A deliberate condition, orchestrated by the church papals to render Europe free once and for all of all African and Asian influence. They ordered the pillage and then destruction of all of their temples, mystery schools, universities and libraries. African (and other) clerics were tried for heresy, many were crucified, burned, or murdered, catapulting Europe into abysmal darkness for more than 500 years. Now, with the memory slate of new generations of peasants wiped clean, it became convenient for the Church to perpetrate its brand of Christianity on to the unsuspecting, ignorant masses. They were even more successful in convincing all of Europe into believing and perpetuating the stories circulated by the inquisitors "explorers" and Jesuits concerning African serpent-centered religious practices. Particularly those of the fiercely autonomous African priestesses, whom they referred to as "*immoral, temple prostitutes,*" condemned so bitterly by the Hebrew biblical patriarchs.

In one propagandistic campaign, the following rumor was widely believed and became a popular folk chant:

At night, the men and women
as well as The Sibyl turn into horrifying snakes.
And whoever wants to enter the cave must first
share lascivious pleasures with those revolting serpents."[5]

Europe was finally "free." Areas where some vestiges of Sibyl or Isis' tradition remained, those worshipers fell prey to ostracism, violence and ridicule. One major object of their wrath was a Sibyl in Norcia, Italy, who apparently refused to relinquish her divine rights or to submit to papal control. She became the town folks quintessential "black victim," and often harassed and taunted with the above chant. She was taunted and jeered as a *"crazed, wretched parasite"*, who "held *orgies with animals*," particularly the *serpent*.

This stereotypic, racist, euro-model of African spirituality serves not only to justify African and Diaspora oppression and under representation in the global and political markets, but more importantly, it serves to obscure the ecclesiastical origins of the papacy and those of the "virgin," Sibyls. Even today, those African nations who continue to resist conversion will suffer the same fate as *Togo, Benin* and *Haiti* who dare dignify *"Voodoo"* as their national religion. Some suspect, that this defiant act of ancestral and deific respect may have even cost former president of Haiti, Aristide his presidency.[6]

Blaming the *"Voodoo"* and all African spiritual traditions as the primary culprit for Africa's and Diaspora economic and social woes, is an old worn colonial tactic, mastered by the Church, supported and reinforced by Western pseudo-rationalist philosophy, and racist propaganda. Its primary and ultimate goal is to spiritually disempower Africans by culturally and theologically perverting their religions, and to discourage their mass appeal to outsiders anywhere in the New World.

NOTES

1.Zacks,p. 327. In earlier times, when the Hellenistic (branch of the Doric) tribes, who would later be known as the Greeks, arrived at the Isle of Crete, (100-67 BC), it was already a powerfully thriving matriarchy, inhabited for centuries by Afro-Ionians (African and Dravidian mixed people), known as *Minoans* and later *Mycenaeans*.

2. Higgins, Vol I. p. 274.

3. Fergusson, p. 3, 12. 14.; Temple, p. 198. This was accomplished mainly through their oracular priestesses who would later establish centers of worship all throughout what became known as the Mycenæ regions, including Dodona, (Mt. Tomaros), Delphi, (Mt. Parnassus), Omphalos, (Thenæ), and
Delos (Mt. Cyntus), During their initial invasions, the Greeks, began a campaign of exterminating the Mycenaeans, and all vestiges of their Serpent-Worshiping *"heathenism"*. Earlier Greek mythology is replete with tales of their destruction of serpents and of the *"serpent races*," who brought them, It was not until the warlike Greeks took notice of the accurate prophesies of these black Mycenæ Sibyl priestesses, and witnessed the miraculous healing powers of these divine serpents, that widespread acceptance and popularity of them permeated Greek culture, and were included in their myths and religious iconography. The most popular being that of the black Scythian, Herakles, whom himself a priest of the serpent Goddess, Echidna. Myths abound hailing his exploits of conquest and of the destruction of the so-called "serpents of darkness," which meant "black *female power*."

4. Ibid. p. 12-13.;Stone, p. 180-197.

5. Zacks,p. 327.

6. In profiling Aristide's forced exile, Fox News, immediately aired a propagandistic mini-documentary on *"Voodoo*," blaming it for Haiti's *"ignorance, poverty and despair*." Never once mentioning that the first black Republic in the Western Hemisphere is still being punished for daring to defeat the military might of the British, French and the U.S. via the supernatural aid of their African gods and ancestors; derisively known as "Voodoo."

CHIEF HOUNON- AMENGANSIE PRIESTESS

Mama Zogbé

Mama Zogbé (legal name, Vivian Hunter-Hindrew) is a fully initiated *Hounon-Amengansie* (High Priestess) of the Amengansie, Ancestral Tchamba, West African Vodoun, Mami Wata, and Afa (Ifa) healing traditions. She resides in the United States, where she maintains her ancestral shines and works full-time as an Amengansie Vodoun priestess and godmother.

Mama Zogbé, African-American

Born from the womb of Mami Wata and the Vodoun, Mama Zogbé's spiritual lineage descends directly from both sides of her maternal and paternal great grandmothers and fathers, who were Mami Wata & Vodoun priests, captured & enslaved as hired-out masons and carvers in Louisiana. During Slavery and Reconstruction, African descendants were forbidden to practice their ancestral religions, many were persecuted and murdered. Such was the case in the family of Mama Zogbé where her great-grandfather, *Prince Hunter,* was killed in Natchitoches, Parish in Louisiana. Family lore recounts that he refusing to convert to Christianity, was chased into a barn and set-ablaze.

131

Over time, the Vodoun tradition was forced underground and a deliberate process of mockery and racist malignment began in American media, religious and educational institutions, creating some of the most perverse, undeserved and enduring stereotypes of African religions, which has continued unabated until the present.

After more than 30 years of intense manifestational encounters, and personal suffering, Mama Zogbé received her first ceremonies in Togo West Africa, by Hounon Togbui (Master), Akuete Durchbach (1988), and full initiations by Hounons Togbuis Arita & Daniel Sossah In Togo, and the U.S. (1996). She completed her final series of ceremonies as Chief Hounon Amengansie in 2003-2005.

As a full-lineage African-American priestess, Mama Zogbé is the first to initiate many in the Diaspora to Mami Wata, Mama Tchamba, Vodoun and Amengansie tradition. She is a graduate of Chaminade University (Honolulu, HI,1981, BGS), and Augusta State University (GA: 1995 M.Ed.). She is world traveled (South America, France, Italy, Czechoslovakia, Germany, Austria, Mexico, Ghana, Cote d'Ivoire, and others). She has been traveling to Togo, West Africa regularly since 1988.

Mama Zogbe is also the founder and president of the first non-profit, 501(c)3, **Mami Wata Healing Society of North America, Inc.**, (formerly **OATH**: *Organization of African Traditional Healers*), which recently won a long overdue victory with the U.S. Library of Congress, in changing the classification of African Traditional Religions ,from the historically derisive label of *Occult/Satanism* to *African Spirituality, Religion, and African-American Studies.* Her hopes that her two-volume well researched book: *Mami Wata: An Ancient African God/dess Unveiled"* can be used as an instrument to shed much needed history and accurate knowledge on African ancient traditional religions and their crucial but long omitted role in laying the theological, ritual and cultural foundation of the major religions throughout the ancient world.

TO REQUEST SPEAKING ENGAGEMENTS PLEASE VISIT

www.mamiwata.com/speaker.html

P.O. Box 211281 * Martinez, GA 30907
Chief Hounon-Amengansie, Mama Zogbé. Main Shrine: (706) 267-3324   Apokassii, Hounon-Amengansie: (678) 358-0620
Fax: (706) 267-3324* Website: www.mamiwata.com

Mami Wata Healers Society of North America

®

Presents

Order
Now!

Other educational books by Mama Zogbé

Volume I
ISBN: 978-0-9716-2457-30
ISBN: 0 0-9716245-7-7
565 pages, 6" x 9"
Price: $53.33

Volume II
ISBN: 978-0-9716-2458-
368 pages, 6" x 9"
Price: $30.64

Available online:

http://www.lulu.com/content/982462
http://www.lulu.com/content/983287
Amazon.com

Please contact your local bookstores as
request that they stock these books!

INDEX

calvary.....34,36
canaanite.....15,39,42,60,74,97
canaanites.....15,39,97
cappadocia.....37
carthage.....44,45,79,83
carthaginian.....17,22,45,74
castrated.....75
catacomb.....11,21,41,43,77,83
catholic.....18,64,73,75,76,79
caucasus.....34
cercaphos.....103
cercylas.....103
ceremonial.....35,75
chaldean.....4,11,14,19,20,30,39,44,73,74,81,90
chalybes.....34
chaste.....66
christ.....3,4,6,7,8,11,13,15,16,21,23,36,38,39,41,44,48,49,53,57,59,
60,67,68,69,70,73,74,75,76,78,79,80,81,
82,83,84,85,86,87,88,89,90,91,93,94,95,98,99,102,103,106
christian.....3,4,6,7,8,11,13,15,16,21,23,36,38,39,41,44,48,49,53,57,
59,60,67,68,69,70,73,74,75,76,79,80,81,
82,83,84,85,86,87,88,89,90,93,95,98,99,103,106
christianity.....3,11,16,36,53,57,60,84,87,90,98,99,106
church.....7,8,11,18,36,38,43,53,56,57,58,59,61,64,66,76,77,78,79
,80,81,83,86,87,90,91,92,93,94,95,
97,98,99
claudius.....75,104,105
cleopatra.....44
crucified.....85
crucifixion.....74
cumae.....44,47,67,68,69,70,74
cumean.....6,48,95
cuneiform.....15
cures.....30,46,48
curing.....6,30,48,66
cursed.....92
curses.....83
cushite.....24,67
cushites.....24
cybele.....24,26,32,66,72
cybella.....24
cyclopean.....39
cythera.....29,32
daemons.....89
dahomean.....37
dahomey.....37,51
delos.....5,20,21,23,27,31,32,66
delphi.....5,21,22,23,25,26,27,29,66,68,70,73,83,89

NOTES

----

1. Higgins, Vol. I. p. 615, 627-628.;Temple, p. 181 ("first fruits". Still performed as "Agbandoto" in Togo, and by Mami Wata Healing Society in Augusta, GA).

2. Hyatt M. H. "Hoodoo-Conjuration-Witchcraft-Rootwork" (Illinois: Alama Egan Hyatt Foundation, 1973), Vols. I-V. p. I.

3. Ibid.

4. Ciholas, Paul. "The Omphalos and the Cross: Pagans and Christians in Search of a Divine Center." Macon: Mercer University Press, 2003. p. 162.

5. Neuman, E. "The Great Mother." (New Jersey: Princeton University Press, 1991.) p. 135-136.; Smith, G. "Chaldean Account of Genesis. " (Montana: Kessinger, 1876). p. 58.

6. The History of Herodotus, 440 B.C.EE., Book V.; see also Temple p. 194

7. Ibid.

8. Temple, Robert. "The Sirius Mystery" (United Kingdom: Arrow Pub., 1999). p. 195.

9. Higgins, Higgins, Godfrey. "Anacalypsis,: An Attempt to Draw Aside the Veil of the Saitic Isis or Inquiry into the origin of Languages, Nations and Religions," Vol. I,II, (Montana: Kessinger Publishing Co., [1836]). Vol 2., p. 328, Vol I. p. n.591.

10. Monterio, M., White, A.C. "As David and the Sibyls Say." (Montana: Kessinger, 1905). p. 159.
Graves, R. "The Greek Myths "Vol. 1&2. New York: Penguin Putnam Inc., 1960.
Greek Myths 1. p. 18.3.

11.Ibid. p. 75.; Bell, John. "Bell's New Pantheon or Historical Dictionary of the Gods, Demi Gods, Heroes and Fabulous Personages of Antiquity Vol. I. II." London: British Library, Strand, 1790. p. 204.;"The Living Bible Paraphrased." Wheaton: Tyndall House Publishers Inc., 1971. I Sam: 28.;Ciholas. p. 129.
Webster's II: New Revised Dictionary," (New York: Berkley Book, 1984) p. 642.;
Webster's New Collegiate Dictionary. P. 1077 (see also: The Oxford Compact Dictionary. Oxford University Press. Second Edition, 2003.

12. Ibid.; Ciholas, Paul. The Omphalos and the Cross: Pagans and Christians in Search of a Divine Center. Macon: Mercer University Press, 2003. p. 123;132.

13. Higgins, Vol I. p. 189,422,585,599.;Ciholas, p. 127,132-133n.11,154.;,Lederer, Wolfgang, M.D., "The Fear of Women" (New York: Grune & Stratton, 1968). p.151,152.

14. Graves, Greek Myths 1. p. 105.; Monterio, p.150.;Bell 130. The Sibyls shrines and temples were located all throughout the known world, including Kemet (Egypt), Libya, Greece, Sparta, Persia, Peloponnesus (Turkey) the Minoan and Ionian Islands, Rome etc.,.

15. see note 6

16. Monteiro, p. 161; Stone. Merlin. "When God Was A Woman" (New York: Barnes & Noble Books, 1993). 112.

17. The word *"Garmantes"* is also a variation of *"Coromanti and Kormantin, Gourmantché,"* which are English and Dutch equivalents,referring to the *now* present day *Guan, Ga-Adangbe clans of N. Ghana and the Anlo-Ewe near Elmina,* and the *Gur* groups of Burkino Faso. Dr. J.D. Elder. *African Survivals. p. 15.; Encyclopedia Brit. Micro. Vol. III. 1976, p. 455-456.;Graves,* The Greek Myths, I. p. 45. *pottery shards date the black Libyan arrival as early as 4,000 B.C.E; The White Goddes. p. 177.;* Temple, p. 244. Black, matriarchal clans were already in an advance stage of civilization 3000 years before the arrival and cultural assimilation of the Dorian (mixed-race) Greeks, Persians and Turks. *Jealousy of these black matriarchs power and prosperity is what prompted the patriarchal invasions.;Briffault Robert. "The Mothers: The matriarchal theory of social origins*" (New York: Grosset & Dunlap, 1963)., *p. 66,66.* Although Briffault has made the same historical error as earlier European researchers in classifying the ancient North Africans and Libyans as *"white,"* he does make their connection to the *Mycenaean* cultures of Asia Minor.

18. Webster's New Collegiate Dictionary, 1977, p. 1076.

19. Ibid. Temple, p. 174.

20. *Briffault, p. 103.*

21. Diner, Helen. *"Mothers and Amazons: The First Feminine History of Culture."*(New York: Double Day Anchor Press, 1973. p. 192,190-191.

22. Horton, p. 224-232.; Ibid. *Encyclopedia Brit. Micro. Vol. VIII. 1976, p. 892-893.;*Graves, The White Goddess," p. 447.; Sappho, known since antiquity to have been the single major influence on Western poetry and literature, inspiring the works of *Tennyson* and others, was hailed as the *"Queen of Poetry." Sappho,"* was born on the Greek Island of *Lesbos (Levsos),* in the town of *Eresus* (610-c. 580 B.C.E). However, she actually grew-up in *Mitylene.* Described as a *"small, dark body filled with immortal fire,"* she wrote her name in her own Afro-Aeolic dialect as *"Psappho."*She was considered the greatest literary poetess of her time, and some have even argued *"of all ages."* She spoke and wrote in the native Aeolian dialect, and her poetry was written in what would be called today, a *"street vernacular style."* Born from an aristocratic family, this black, educated women enjoyed "hanging out" with the ladies on the island of Lesbos, holding poetry circles, that she founded. Although Psappho was married (Cercylas) and had birthed a daughter (Cleis), her poetry centered on intense erotic amours with other women. In her poetry she also expressed her fears, hatred and jealousies just as equally against her rivals and enemies. During the Middle Ages, the books that survived the Inquisitions, were completely destroyed. Only quotes of two long poems, and few single-line fragments have been preserved. In spite of Graves resentment of the *"Attic comedians who caricature her as an insatiable Lesbian,"* Psappho is still hailed as a s/hero to the black lesbian communities, and to others, who view her as an exemplar during a time when the barbarity of Christian patriarchy had concealed and destroyed their S/heros.

23. Horton, George. *Home of the Nymphs & Vampires: The Isles of Greece.* Indianapolis:Bobbs-Merrill Company, 1929, p. 282-283. Higgins, p. 435.;*Encyclopedia Brit. Micro. Vol. V. 1976, p. 410-411.*

24. Ibid. p. 259.; Higgins, p. 456, Rhodes was one of ten islands known collectively as "the *Dodecanese.*" (a Greek word "dodeka and nesos", meaning *ten islands*).After the patriarchal incursion, it was later known as the *"Bride of the Sun,* and "Land of the Roses." The sun was said to be named after the black Egyptian *"Cercaphos,"* who was the *"daughter of the Sun."*

25. Horton, p. 86.

26. Ibid. p. 87.

27. Ibid. p. 86
28. Ibid. p. 88.
29. *Horton, p. 88,282.;Encyclopedia Brit. Micro. Vol. III. 1976, p. 451-452;*. Bell, p. 127-
30. Higgins, Vol I. p. 227.
31.Higgins, Vol I. p. 709.
32. Brown JNR., p. 78,Higgins, p. Vol I. p. 364, 702, Vol II. p. 768-769
33. Diner, p. 188-190.; see Bibliography for "on-line notes" *'Lycian Turkey: The Federalist Papers'.*;Osei, Osafo. K . *"A Discourse on Akan Perpetual Calendar."* Accra: Ghana, 199, p. *xiii.*
34. Ibid.
35. Ibid., p. 188.
36. *Encyclopedia Brit. Micro. Vol. V. 1976, p. 706-707.*;Smith, p. 41.
37. Bulwer-Lytton. Sir Eward, Bart. *"The Last Days of Pompeii."* London: A.L. Burt Company, Publishers, 1850, p. 207.
38. Ibid, p. 58; Bell, p. 247.
39. Monteiro, p. 24,75.;Higgins, p. 812-813.
40. Lederer, p.151,152.;Ciholas, p. 127,133-134,138,140, 157.
41. Monterio, p. 13,16-17.; Bell Vol. II, p.121.;Graves, *I Claudius.*
42 Lederer, p. 170-171.; Frazer, p. 348.; Higgins, Vol. I. p. 137.;Encyclopedia Britannica. Micropaedia. Ready Reference. 15th ed., 1974, Vol. I. p.649.
43. Bell, Vol. II. p. 121.
44. Ibid., 121.
45. Ciholas, p. 142,136
46 Herodotus, Book V.;Graves. Greek Myths. Vol 2, p.162.
47. Ibid. p. 150.
48. Ibid. 153.
49. *"The Living Bible Paraphrased."* Wheaton: Tyndall House Publishers Inc., 1971. I Sam. 28:6; 28:13. DiGivry, p. 167.; Lederer, p.151.; Frazer. p. 3.; Ciholas. p. 127,161.
50. Monterio, p. 84,172.
51. Ibid.,136.
52. Bell, p. Vol II. 122.
53.Stone, p.55,165-166.; Lederer, p. 157,159,169.;Graves, Greek Myths 2. p.190.;Walker, p.30-31.
54. *Encyclopedia Brit. Micro. Vol. III. 1976, p. 455-456.*;Graves, The Greek Myths, I. p. 45. ; *The White Goddes. p. 177.*; Temple, p. 244..;Briffault, p. 66,66.
55.Walker, p. 46-47.
56. Ciholas,p.131.: Terry,Vol. III. p. 1023-31.
57. Ciholas, p. 123, 125.; Lederer, p. 149, 152, 158-159.
58. Terry, Milton. S. *The Sibylline Oracles.* Translated From the Greek into English Black Verse. New York: Eaton & Mains, 1899.;Monteiro, M., White, A.C. *As David and the Sibyls Say.* Montana: Kessinger,1905.;Graves, Robert. *"The White Goddess."* Amended and Enlarged Edition.(New York: Farrar, Strass, and Giroux,1980), p105,228, 254.;Higgins,Vol.I,167,427,519,540,563-566,574,613,634-637,663,666,671.;Bell, John. *Bell's New Pantheon or Historical Dictionary of the Gods, Demi Gods, Heroes and Fabulous Personages of Antiquity* Vol. I. II. London: British Library, Strand, 1790, p.234-237.;Stone, Merlin. *"When God Was A Woman"* (New York: Barnes & Noble Books, 1993), p. 211.;Frazer, James, G. Sir. *"The Golden Bough: A study in magic and religion"* (New York: The Macmillan Co., 1943), Vol I., p. 3,348.;Temple, Robert. *"The Sirius Mystery"* (United Kingdom: Arrow Pub., 1999), p. 172,178, 194-195.
59. Monteiro. p. 40.

60. Ibid. p. 100.

61. Ibid.

62. Graves, Greek Myths, Vol 2. p. 131.; (see also *"Gargars"* link in On-Line Resources,).

63.Stone, p.55, 165-166.; Lederer, p. 157,159,169.;Graves, Greek Myths 2. p. 190.;Walker, p.30-31.

64. Ibid. p. 73.

65. Graves, *Greek Myths*, p. 28-29.;Monteiro, p. 73.Graves, *White Goddess*, p. 336.

66. Monterio. p. 160-161, 164-165.

67.Neuman,p.218.;Higgins,p.264,332,333,456.;Stone,p.88-93,151,204-205.;207-211.;Walker,p.502-503.;Graves,Greek Myths 1. p. 28.2,31c,32.1,33,35.5,38.1 & 38.4, 45,47.131.2,131.4,135.3; Graves.The White Goddess, p. 316,356.

68. Bell, p. 135.

69. Ciholas, p. 131.; Graves, Vol I.p. 51. 53

70. Lederer, p. 149.; Bell, p. 177.; Graves, p. 390.

71. Monteiro, p. 9.

72. Ibid. p. 9-10.

73. Monteiro, p. 6.

74. Tirmizi, p. 1.

75. Bell, p.95.

76 .Monterio. p 154.

77. Monteiro, p. 161, 148, 24, 91.

78. Monteiro, p. 25,27.: Bell 235.

79. Graves. *I Claudius*, p. 6.

80. Smith, p. 37.

81. Monteiro, p. 160-161.

82. Clifton, p. 98-99

83. Ibid: Encycl. Brit. Vol VI, p. 1012-13.

84. Ibid. p. 191.

85. Bell. p. 124-125,235-237.

86. Temple,p.237.: Waljer, p. E.W.S., p. 208.

87. Ciholas, p. 125- 126.:Bell, p.124-125.:Walker, p. 208.

88. Temple, p. 237.

89. Higgins, Vol I. p. 190.

90.Bell. p. 236.

91. Monterio. p. 12.

92. Monterio, p. 44 : Bell, p. 236.: Ciholas, p. 134,137.

93. Ciholas, p. 138.

94. Ibid. p. 139.

95. Abraham was a diviner and Shepard from the black, East African clan of the *Korites*, meaning worshipers of Isis in her grain and fecundity aspect as the goddess Kore. Mohammed built his tradition from these long established black, matriarchal worshipers of the black goddess *Al-lat (Awussa)*, who have now been reduced to his *"daughters."*

96. Hammer, p. 61.

97. Higgings, Vol I. p. 59, 243,586.

98.Ibid. p. 158-159,253,429.

99. Monteiro, p. 99.

100. Ciholas, p. 1146-47, 150.;Walker, p. 1102.; Barnstone, p. 501-502,555-561.

101. Monteiro. p. 11. 13.

102. Ciholas, p. 162

103. Ibid.

104. Lederer, p. 151.
105. DeGivry, p. 167.
106. Ciholas, p. 140-141.
107.Monteiro. p. 103.

BIBLIOGRAPHY

Ancient All-Woman Cult Remains Mystery." San Antonio Express News. May 5, 1985, 16A.

Bastide. R. *"African Civilizations in the New World."* New York: Harper Torchbooks, 1971.

Bell, John. *"Bell's New Pantheon or Historical Dictionary of the Gods, Demi Gods, Heroes and Fabulous Personages of Antiquity Vol. I. II."* London: British Library, Strand, *1790.*

Bernal, M. "Black Athena: *The afroasiatic roots of classical civilization*" (New Jersey: Rutgers University Press, 1987).

Black, Jeremy, Green, Anthony. *"Gods, Demons and Symbols of Ancient Mesopotamia. An Illustrated Dictionary."* Austin: University of Texas Press, 1992.

Briffault, Robert. "*The Mothers: The matriarchal theory of social origins*" (New York: Grosset & Dunlap, 1963).

Brown, Robert, JNR. *"Poseidon."* London: Longmans Green, and Co., 1872.

Bulwer-Lytton. Sir Eward, Bart. *"The Last Days of Pompeii*" (London: A.L. Burt Company, Publishers, 1850).

Bussagli, Marco (Editor). "*Rome: Art & Architecture*" (Cologne: Könemann Verlagesgesellschaft mbH, 1999).

Ciholas, Paul. *"The Omphalos and the Cross: Pagans and Christians in Search of a Divine Center."* Macon: Mercer University Press, 2003.

Childress, David. H. "*Lost Cities & Ancient Mysteries of Africa & Arabia*" (Illinois: Adventures Unlimited Press, 1984).

Clark, Hyde and Wake, Staniland C. *"Serpent and Siva Worship"* (New York: J.W. Bouton, 1877). Reprinted by Kesslinger Publishing, LLC.

Clarke, John, Henrik. *"African Warrior Queens"* (ed. Ivan Van Sertima, Black Women in Antiquity). (New Jersey: Transaction Publishers, 2002), 123-134.

Clifton, Chas, S. *"Encyclopedia of Heresies and Heretics."* New York: Barns & Noble, 1992.

Dalley, S. *"Myths From Mesoptotamia. Creation, The Flood, Gilgamesh, and Others."* (Oxford: University Press, 2000).

Darkwah, Nana. B. *"The Africans Who Wrote The Bible: Ancient secrets Africa and Christianity have never told"* (Maryland: Aduana Publishing, 2002).

Givry, Emile Grillot de. *"Picture Museum of Sorcery, Magic & Alchemy."* University Press. New Hyde Park, New York. 1963.

Diner, Helen. *"Mothers and Amazons: The First Feminine History of Culture"* (New York: DoubleDay Anchor Press, 1973).

Diop, A.C. *"The African Origin of Civilization"* (West Port: Lawrence Hill & Co., 1974).

Encyclopedia Britannica. (London: Encyclopedia Britannica, Inc.), Vol. 6, 8. 15th ed., 1974.

Macropedia. (London: Encyclopedia Britannica, Inc.), Vols. I, III, IV, VII, VIII, X. 15th ed., 1974.

—,Knowledge in Depth, (London: Encyclopedia Britannica, Inc.) Vol 8, 1974.

Falkener Edward. *"Ephesus and the Temple of Diana."* (London: Day & Son, Gate Street, Lincoln's-Inn Fields, Lithographers to the Queen, 1862). Reprinted by Kessinger Publisher's.

148

Fergusson, James, Esq., F.R.S., M.R.A.S., "Tree and Serpent Worship: Illustrations of myth and art in India in the first and fourth centuries after Christ" (London: India Museum of London, 1868).

Field. M.J. "Angels and Ministers of Grace." An anthropologist Finds Striking Parallels Between Events Observed in Contemporary African Villages and Those Recorded in Ancient Biblical Narratives. (New York: Hill and Wang, 1971).

Floyer, Sir John. "The Sibylline Oracles." Translated from the Best Greek Copies, and compar'd with the Sacred Prophesies, especially with Daniel and the Revelations. (London: R. Bruges, for J. Nicholson, 1713).

Forlong, J.G.R. Rivers of Life or Sources and Streams of the Faiths of Man in all lands Showing the Evolution of Faiths from the Rudest Symbolisms to the Latest Spiritual Developments. London: Bernard Quaritch, Vol I & II, 1883.

Frazer, James, G. Sir. "The Golden Bough: A study in magic and religion" (New York: The Macmillan Co., 1943), Vol I.

Freed, Rita. E. "Ramesses The Great: The pharaoh and his time." (Charlotte: Mint Museum of Art, 1987).

Gokovali, Sadan, "EPHESUS", Ticaret Matbaacilik, Izmir, Turkey.

Graves, Robert. "I Claudius." New York: Vintage Books, 1961.

__ "Claudius The God." New York: Vintage Books, 1962.

__ "The White Goddess." Amended and Enlarged Edition. (New York: Farrar, Strass, and Giroux, 1980).

—. "The Greek Myths "Vol. 1&2. New York: Penguin Putnam Inc., 1960.

Gubernatis, Angelo de. "Zoological Mythology or the Legends of Animals Vol. 2," New York: MacMillan & Co., 1872.

Hambly, Wildred, D., Serpent Worship in Africa. Anthropological Ser. Vol XXI, No. 1. Pub. 289. (Chicago: Field Museum Press, 1931).

Hammer, Michael F. et. al., "Y Chromosomes of Jewish Priests." (Nature – Volume 385 –2 January 1997. (See on-line resources).

Higgins, Godfrey. *"Anacalypsis,: An Attempt to Draw Aside the Veil of the Saitic Isis or Inquiry into the origin of Languages, Nations and Religions,"* Vol. I,II, (Montana: Kessinger Publishing Co., [1836]).

— 'Celtic Druids,' (Montana: Kessinger Publishing Co.) [Orginally published 1829, London: St. Paul Chruchyard.]

Hinz, Walther. *"The Lost World of Elam: Re-creation of a Vanished Civilization."* (New York: New York University Press, 1973).

Horton, George. *"Home of the Nymphs & Vampires: The Isles of Greece."* (Indianapolis:Bobbs-Merrill Company, 1929).

Inman,Thomas. *"Ancient Pagan and Modern Christian Symbolism: with an Essay on Baal Worship, on the Assyrian Sacred Grove and other Allied Symbols."* (Montana:Kessinger Publishing, 1915).

Jackson, John, G. *"Ethiopia And The Origin of Civilization"* (Maryland: Black Classic Press, 1985).

Kindler, B. Babaji. *"Twenty-four Aspects of Mother Kali."* (Portland: SRV Association of Oregon, 1996).

Lanciani, R. *"Pagan & Christian Rome."* (Boston & New York: Houghton, Mifflin and Company, 1896).

Lapatin, Kenneth. "Mysteries of the Snake Goddess: Art, Desire, And the Forging of History." (Cambridge: Da Capo Press, 2003).

Lederer, Wolfgang, M.D., *"The Fear of Women"* (New York: Grune & Stratton, 1968).

Lee, Henry. "Sea Fables Explained." (London: William Clowns and Sons, Limited, 1883).

Lesko, Barbara S. *"The Great Goddesses of Egypt"* (Oklahoma: University of Oklahoma Press, 1999).

---. *"Women's Earliest Records: From Ancient Egypt and Western Asia."* In: Brown Judaic Studies, Georgia Scholars Press, (1987) 166.

Lewis. I.M. *"Ecstatic Religion.."* *An Anthropological Study of Spirit*

Possession and Shamanism." (Great Britain: Hazell Watson & Viney Ltd, 1971).

Life. "The World's Great Religions." (New York: Time Incorporated, 1957).

Lindsay, Jack. "Origins of Astrology" (New York: Barnes & Noble, Inc, 1971).

Lucas, Olumide. J. "Religions in West Africa and Ancient Egypt" (Lagos: Nigerian National Press, 1970).

Markoe, Glenn. ed. "Petra Rediscovered: Lost City of the Nabataeans." (New York: Harry N. Abrams, Inc., Cincinnati Art Museum. 2003).

Massey, Gerald. "Ancient Egypt: The light of the world" (Montana: Kessinger Publishing Co.), Vols. I & II.

---. "A Book of the Beginnings" (New York: A & B Publishers, 1994).

Meeks, Dimitri and Christine Favard. "Daily Life of the Egyptian Gods" (New York: Cornell University Press, 1996).

Metzner, Ralph. "Black Goddess And Other Mythic Earth Images" (Rochester, NY:Green Psychology, Inner Traditions International, 1999).

Milton, Terry. "The Sibylline Oracles" (New York: Eaton & Mains, 1899).

Monteiro, M., White, A.C. "As David and the Sibyls Say." (Montana: Kessinger, 1905).

Neumann, E. "The Great Mother." (New Jersey: Princeton University Press, 1991.)

"Vatican,' Newsweek, 1968.

Museums Rome," Newsweek, 1968.

"Cairo," Newsweek, 1969.

"Museums of Egypt," Newsweek, 1980.

'Pompeii and its Museums,' Newsweek, 1979.

'Lovre, Paris, Newsweek, 1967.

Nicholson, Paul, Shaw, Ian. "British Museum Dictionary of Ancient Egypt." (London: The Bristish Museum Company Ltd., 1995).

Oliver, G. Rev. *History of Initiation.* (Montana: Kessinger, (1855).

Oppert, Jules. *"Expédition en Mesopotamie",* Études Assyriennes, 200-16.

Panati, Charles. *"Sacred Origins of Profound Things"* (New York: Penguin Books, 1996).

Rajasingham K.T. *"Historical Survey of Eelam."* *Weekend Express* (April 24, 1999).

Redd, Danita. *"Black Madonna of Europe: Diffusion of the African Isis."* African Presence in Early Europe. (ed.) Sertima. (Brunswick: Transaction Books, 1987),108-133.

Rutherford, M.L. *"Truths of History"* (Athens: Georgia, 1920).

Saggs, H.W.F. *"Civilization Before Greece and Rome"* (New Haven: Yale University Press, 1969).

Scobie, Edward., The Moors and Portugal's Global Expansion. Rashidi, Runoko. (ed.) "African Presence in Early Asia." Co-Edited by Ivan Van Sertima. (New Brunswick: Transaction Publishers, 2002)

Seifert, Charles, C. *"The Negro's or Ethiopian's Contribution to Art"* (Baltimore: Black Classic Press, 1938).

Sertima, Ivan. V. (ed.) *"African Presence in Early Europe"* (New Jersey: Transaction Books, 1987).

Sertima, Ivan V. (ed.) *"Golden Age of the Moor"* (New Brunswick: Transaction Publishers, 2002).

—,(ed.) *"Black Women in Antiquity"* (New Brunswick: Transaction Publishers, 2002).

Sitchin, Z. *"Divine Encounters: A guide to visions, angels, and other emissaries"* (New York: Avon Books, 1995).

Shaw,Ian, Nicholson, Paul. *"British Museum Dictionary of Ancient Egypt."* (London: British Museum Company Ltd., 1995).

Smith, G. *"Chaldean Account of Genesis. "* (Montana: Kessinger, 1876).

Spek, Van der, Bert. "The atammus of Esagila in the Seleucid and Arsacid Periods" (ed.) Joachim Marzahn, Hans Neumann. Assyriologica et Semitica. M·nster: Festschrift f·r Joachim Oelsner (2000), 437-446.

Stone, Merlin. *When God Was A Woman* (New York: Barnes & Noble Books, 1993).

Suther, D. Judith. *"The Gorgon Medusa,"* South, 165-177.

Jonathan, D. Evans. *"The Dragon,"* South, 28-55.

Sitchin, Z. *"The Cosmic Code. The Earth Chronicles"* (New York: Avon, 1978), No. 6.

Steindorff, George and Seele, Keith. C. *"When Egypt Ruled The East"* (Chicago: University of Chicago Press, 1999).

"Out of Africa: The Superb Artwork of Ancient Nubia," Washington: *Smithsonian* 1993: 90-101.

Temple, Robert. *"The Sirius Mystery"* (United Kingdom: Arrow Pub., 1999).

Terry, Milton. S. *"The Sibylline Oracles. Translated From the Greek into English Black Verse."* (New York: Eaton & Mains, 1899).

Thorsten, Geraldine. *"God Herself: The feminine roots of astrology"* (New York, Avon, Books, 1981).

Thorsten, Geraldine. *"God Herself: The feminine roots of astrology"* (New York, Avon, Books, 1981).

"The Living Bible Paraphrased" (Wheaton: Tyndall House Publishers Inc., 1971).

"Unger's Bible Handbook." (Chicago: Moody Press, 1966.)

Wake, Staniland C. *"Sacred Prostitution & Marriage by Capture'."* (New York: The Big Dollar Book, 1932).

Walker, B. G. *The I Ching of the Goddess* (Massachusetts: Fair Winds Press, 1999).

Walker, B. G. *The Women's Encyclopedia of Myths and Secrets* (New York: Harper & Row, 1983).

"Webster's II: *New Revised Dictionary*," (New York: Berkley Book, 1984).

"Webster's New Collegiate Dictionary." (Massachusetts: G.& C. Merriam Company, 1977).

Winters, Clyde A. *"The Proto-Culture of the Dravidians ,Manding and Sumerians."* Tamil Civilization 3, no.1: (1985a).

Winter, Clyde A. *"The Genetic Unity Between the Dravidian ,Elamite, Manding and Sumerian Languages."* p Sixth ISAS ,1984, (Hong Kong: Asian Research Service, 1985d).

---, '*"Tamil, Sumerian and Manding and the Genetic Mode."* International Journal of Dravidian Linguistics, 1985.

---, *"Trade Between East Africa and Ancient China."* Afrikan Mwalimu 4, No. 3 (1978).

---, *"The Relationship of Afrikans and Chinese in the Past."* Afrikan Mwalimu (Jan 1979): 25-31.

---, *"Blacks in Ancient China. Pt. 1: The Founders of Xia and Shang."* Journal of Black Studies (1984): 8-13.

"The Genetic Unity Between the Dravidian ,Elamite, Manding and Sumerian Languages." p Sixth ISAS ,1984, (Hong Kong: Asian Research Service, 1985d).

Zacks, Richard. *"An Underground Education"* (New York: Doubleday, 1997).

Printed in Great Britain
by Amazon

16978358R00091